I0074050

NURSING
WEALTHY

NURSING WEALTHY: Transform Your Career, Build Lasting Wealth, and Lead with Purpose

Copyright © 2025 by Mary Ghazarian

This is a work of creative nonfiction. Some parts have been fictionalized to varying degrees, for various purposes. The events and conversations in this book have been set down to the best of the author's ability, although some names and details have been changed to protect the privacy of individuals.

All rights reserved. No part of this book may be reproduced or used in any manner without written permission of the copyright owner except for the use of quotations in a book review.

The author and publisher of this book have used their best efforts in preparing this material. While every attempt has been made to verify the information provided in this book, neither the author nor the publisher assumes any responsibility for errors, omissions, inaccuracies, or results attained upon applying the contents of the book

The author and publisher or any other contributor to this book shall in no event be liable for any loss, or other damages, including, but not limited to special, incidental, consequential or other damages. As always, the direct and specific advice of a competent professional that specializes in the reader's specific circumstances should be sought. Investment and business advice is educational and not personalized. No results are guaranteed.

For information about special discounts for bulk purchases or other inquiries visit: www.maryghazarian.com

Cover and Interior design by Olivier Darbonville

ISBN 978-1-7390513-4-1 (hardcover)
ISBN 978-1-7390513-3-4 (softcover)
ISBN 978-1-7390513-5-8 (ebook)

NURSING
WEALTHY

TRANSFORM YOUR CAREER, BUILD LASTING WEALTH, AND LEAD WITH PURPOSE

MARY GHAZARIAN MN, NP-PHC

DEDICATION

To every nurse who has ever felt trapped between their calling to care and their need to thrive.

To my two sons, who have redefined worth for me and remind me daily that caring for others and building wealth aren't opposites, but partners in creating the life you want to live. May you grow up in a world where nurses are valued not just for their hearts, but for their minds, their business acumen, and their unlimited potential.

To my husband, whose unwavering support made every late night of writing, every moment of doubt, and every leap of faith possible. You believed in this vision before I did.

To the nurses who will read this book and choose transformation, you are the revolution healthcare has been waiting for. The world needs nurses who operate from abundance, advocate from strength, and lead from positions of financial empowerment.

To my advanced reader team thank you for your time, energy and thoughtful review of the contents of this book.

And finally, to that nurse sitting in a hospital parking garage right now, crying about money and feeling trapped by circumstances beyond your control, everything is about to change. The life you want is not only possible, it's inevitable once you understand that your worth, your expertise, and your potential for wealth are far greater than anyone ever told you.

CONTENTS

INTRODUCTION

What If Everything You've Been Told About Nurses and Money Is Wrong?

Olivia's Story

OLIVIA WALLACE STARED AT THE CEILING OF HER BREAK ROOM, the fluorescent lights buzzing overhead like angry wasps. Her double shift at Metropolis General's ICU had turned into a nightmare—three codes, two family conferences where she'd held sobbing relatives while doctors delivered devastating news, and now Mrs. Christof in bed 7 was asking for the fourth time why her husband wasn't waking up.

It was 2 AM on a Tuesday, and Olivia's body felt like it belonged to someone else. Her feet throbbed in the expensive compression socks she'd splurged on last month, thinking they might make the 12-hour shifts more bearable. They didn't. Nothing did anymore.

She pulled out her phone and scrolled through her banking app—a compulsive habit she'd developed lately. Checking account: $847. Credit card balance: $4,200. The mortgage payment would hit in three days, along with daycare for Madison, her five-year-old daughter who was probably having another nightmare about monsters under her bed. Olivia wouldn't be there to comfort her. Again.

"Another double?" asked Sarah, the night charge nurse, poking her head into the break room. "Girl, you're going to burn yourself out."

Olivia managed a weak smile. "Overtime pays time-and-a-half. Madison needs new school clothes, and we're behind on the car payment."

Sarah shook her head. "You're one of the best ICU nurses we have. Seven years, all those certifications. Shouldn't you be making enough without killing yourself?"

That's what everyone said. *You're a nurse, you have job security. Good benefits. A pension.* What they didn't say was that "good" wasn't enough when you lived in a city where a modest three-bedroom house cost $600,000, when daycare ran $1,800 a month, when every emergency—and there were always emergencies—sent you deeper into debt.

Olivia's husband Mickey worked full-time in construction, but his income fluctuated with the seasons and the economy. They'd done everything right: bought the house they could "afford" according to the bank, budgeted carefully, avoided impulse purchases. But somehow, every month felt like they were drowning a little more.

She closed the banking app and opened Instagram instead, immediately regretting it. There was her nursing school classmate Jessica posting from Bali—her third international trip this year. "Living my best life! #NurseLife #blessed," the caption read. Jessica worked in the ER at a smaller hospital, made less money than Olivia, and was single with no kids. Yet somehow she could afford to jet-set while Olivia was rationing her coffee at home.

The worst part wasn't the money, though. It was the feeling that this was it—that this was all nursing could ever be. Show up, save lives, go home exhausted, repeat. The ICU had been her dream when she was a new grad, the pinnacle of critical care nursing. Now it felt like a prison and the constant beeping was maddening .

"Code blue, room 12. Code blue, room 12." The announcement crackled over the intercom.

Olivia shoved her phone back in her pocket and ran toward room 12, her brain automatically shifting into crisis mode. During the twenty-minute resuscitation effort, she forgot about her bank account, her aching feet, and her daughter's nightmares. She became the nurse she'd trained to be—competent, focused, life-saving.

They got the patient back. His heart rhythm stabilized, his blood pressure climbed, and colour returned to his face. At that moment, Olivia remembered why she'd become a nurse. But as she walked back to the break room an hour later to finish her cold coffee, the weight of her financial stress settled back on her shoulders like a lead blanket.

At 7 AM, she finally clocked out and walked to her ten-year-old Honda Civic in the hospital parking garage. The parking fee was $15 a day—$300 a month just to park at her own workplace. She sat in the driver's seat, too tired to start the engine, and let herself have one moment of complete honesty.

"I can't keep doing this," she whispered to her reflection in the rear-view mirror. "There has to be more."

But what if there wasn't? What if this was just what nursing was—important work that left you broke and exhausted? What if all the talk about "calling" and "making a difference" was just code for "accept less money because you're supposed to care more about service than survival"?

Olivia started the car and drove home through the empty streets, past the coffee shops and boutiques she couldn't afford to shop in, to the house that was slowly suffocating her family's financial future. Mickey would be getting Madison ready for school in a few hours while Olivia slept off another night of holding other people's lives together while her own fell apart.

She pulled into her driveway and sat for another moment, looking at the small house they'd stretched to afford. The dream house, they'd called it when they signed the mortgage papers seven years ago. Just now, it felt more like a nightmare with peeling shingles.

What Olivia didn't know—what no one had ever taught her in nursing school or orientation or the dozens of continuing education courses she'd taken—was that she was sitting on a goldmine of skills and expertise that could transform her financial life completely.

She didn't know that everything she'd been told about nurses and money was wrong. But, she was about to find out.

Why I Chose to Tell Olivia's Story

I could have written this book as a traditional financial guide filled with charts, graphs, and step-by-step instructions. I could have organized it into neat chapters about budgeting, investing, and side hustles, complete with worksheets and calculators.

Instead, I chose to tell you the story of Olivia Wallace—a fictional nurse who represents a composite of every nurse I've coached, every colleague I've worked alongside, and every conversation I've had with financially frustrated healthcare professionals over the past decade.

Olivia isn't real, but her story is. It's built from my own experience of financial stress as a nurse, from the hundreds of coaching clients who've shared their struggles with me, and from interviews with nurses who've found their way to financial independence. Her challenges are the challenges I hear about every day: the overtime trap, the lifestyle inflation, the feeling that despite having an "essential" job, money is always tight.

But Olivia's story doesn't end where the introduction leaves off. Over the course of this book, you'll follow her journey from financial stress to financial empowerment, from feeling trapped by her circumstances to discovering opportunities she never knew existed.

You'll see her grapple with the same limiting beliefs that might be holding you back. You'll watch her make mistakes—some of the same ones I made—and learn from them. You'll witness her transformation from a nurse who feels undervalued and overworked to one who understands her true worth and knows how to claim it.

Most importantly, you'll see that her transformation doesn't require her to abandon her values or stop caring about patients. Instead, you'll discover how financial empowerment actually makes her a better nurse—more present, more confident, more able to advocate fearlessly for what's right.

Why I Wrote This Book

Three years after my own financial crisis—when I was seven months pregnant, tears streaming down my cheeks during a virtual call with the bankruptcy trustee while my two-year-old was safely at grandma's house—I realized I'd been approaching the problem all wrong. For years, I'd been trying to build wealth the way everyone else did, following generic financial advice that ignored the unique realities of nursing.

That advice failed me spectacularly because it didn't account for shift work, emotional labor, the wage ceilings that limit employed nurses' earning potential, or the psychological toll of life-and-death decision-making. I started to feel like nursing should be my side hustle, rather than leaning into it. I treated my nursing expertise as irrelevant to wealth building instead of recognizing it as my greatest financial asset.

But here's what I discovered during my darkest financial hour: while my seven-figure personal training studios were shuttered by pandemic restrictions and driving us deeper into debt, my small nursing-related income streams weren't just surviving—they were thriving. Nurses were reaching out for coaching about advancing their careers. My courses on clinical practice were generating consistent sales. The "side projects" I'd barely paid attention to suddenly became our financial lifeline.

That's when I realized the secret that wealthy nurses know but most never learn: **We've been building wealth in the wrong places while sitting on the ultimate goldmine.**

I wrote this book because I got tired of watching brilliant nurses accept financial limitation as the price of meaningful work. I got tired of seeing nurses work themselves to exhaustion for systems that profit from their dedication while keeping them financially dependent. Most of all, I got tired of the myth that caring and wealth-building are incompatible.

In my first book, *Nursing Wisely: How to Build a Nursing Career That Is Worthwhile, Interesting, Sustainable, Empowered, and Limitless*, I helped nurses create fulfilling careers by putting themselves first. But as

I coached more nurses, I kept encountering the same barrier: financial stress was undermining everything else they were trying to build.

You can have the most meaningful, purposeful nursing career in the world, but if you're worried about paying bills, that worry seeps into everything. Financial stress affects your sleep, your relationships, your ability to be present with patients, and your capacity to make career choices based on passion rather than desperation.

That's when I realized that financial empowerment isn't separate from career fulfillment—it's foundational to it.

This book is my answer to every nurse who has ever felt guilty for wanting financial security, who has ever wondered if there's more possible than living paycheck to paycheck, and who deserves to know their true worth.

Who This Book Is For

This book is for you if:

- You're a nurse who wants financial security without compromising your values
- You feel undervalued financially despite having essential, life-saving skills
- You're tired of working extra shifts just to make ends meet
- You want to build wealth but don't know how your nursing background applies
- You've been told that nurses should be grateful for their "calling" and not focus on money
- You're ready to challenge the belief that financial struggle is noble
- You want to prove that nurses can have both meaningful work AND financial empowerment

Whether you're a new graduate drowning in student loans, a mid-career nurse feeling stuck financially, or an experienced nurse planning for retirement, this book will show you how to leverage your nursing expertise into lasting financial security.

You don't need an MBA or a trust fund or a side business selling essential oils. You need to understand that your nursing skills are wealth-building superpowers disguised as "just doing your job."

What Makes This Different

This isn't another generic financial advice book that treats all professions the same. Traditional financial wisdom assumes you work predictable hours, have stable income, and can think clearly about investments after a calm day at the office.

That advice fails nurses spectacularly.

It doesn't account for shift work that disrupts your sleep and decision-making capacity. It ignores the emotional toll of healthcare work and how compassion fatigue affects your ability to focus on personal finances. It treats your nursing skills as irrelevant to wealth building instead of recognizing them as your greatest financial assets.

This book addresses the unique challenges nurses face while revealing the extraordinary advantages we possess. Your crisis management skills, your ability to work under pressure, your healthcare expertise, your recession-proof career are superpowers waiting to be unleashed.

Every strategy in this book accounts for shift work, patient care responsibilities, and nursing ethics. These aren't generic tactics adapted for nurses—they're wealth-building approaches created by a nurse, for nurses, tested with hundreds of coaching clients and refined over years of implementation.

How to Use This Book

This book is designed to be both inspiration and instruction. Olivia's story will show you what's possible, while my commentary will show you exactly how to make it happen in your own life.

Here's how to get the most from your reading experience:

Read Actively

This isn't a textbook you study once and shelve. It's a transformation guide meant to be marked up, highlighted, and referenced repeatedly. Write in the margins. Dog-ear pages. Make it yours.

Follow Olivia's Journey Chronologically

While you could skip around, Olivia's transformation builds on itself. Each chapter reveals new insights that depend on previous breakthroughs. Trust the process and follow her story from beginning to end.

Complete the Wealth Work Exercises

At the end of each chapter, you'll find reflection questions and practical exercises. These aren't optional—they're how you translate Olivia's insights into your own transformation. Set aside time to work through them thoroughly.

Take Action Between Chapters

Don't just read about Olivia's changes—implement them. If she calculates her true net worth, you calculate yours. If she negotiates her salary, you prepare for your own negotiation. Let her courage inspire your action.

Connect with Other Readers

Share your insights on social media using #NursingWealthy. Join online nursing communities to discuss the concepts. Find an accountability partner who's also working through the book. Transformation happens faster in community and accountability.

Return and Review

Your first read-through will give you the big picture. Your second will reveal details you missed. Your third will show you how far you've come. Plan to revisit this book every six months as you implement these strategies.

Adapt to Your Situation

Olivia's circumstances won't match yours exactly. She's in the ICU; you might be in pediatrics. She has a 5-year-old; you might have teenagers or no kids. Take the principles and adapt them to your unique situation.

Be Patient with the Process

Olivia's transformation happens over months, not days. Your journey will have a similar timeline. Don't expect overnight changes, but do expect consistent progress if you consistently apply what you learn.

Olivia's Journey Becomes Your Roadmap

Throughout this book, you'll follow Olivia through six transformational phases that spell out W-E-A-L-T-H:

W - Wealth Mindset & Whole Net Worth: Olivia discovers she's been calculating her worth all wrong and learns to see the hidden assets she's been overlooking.

E - Energy Management: She stops trading time for money and starts optimizing her most valuable resource—her energy.

A - Asset Building & Strategic Investments: Olivia learns to make her money work as hard as she does, using investment strategies designed for healthcare professionals.

L - Leverage & Scale Your Expertise: She transforms her nursing knowledge into additional income streams that work whether she's clocked in or not.

T - Time Freedom & Financial Independence: Olivia calculates what true freedom looks like and creates a plan to make nursing optional rather than mandatory.

H - Health as Your Foundation: She discovers that protecting her physical and mental health isn't separate from building wealth—it's the foundation that makes everything else possible.

Each section combines Olivia's story with practical strategies, mindset shifts, and action steps you can implement immediately. You'll get the emotional connection of following someone's transformation alongside the practical tools you need to create your own.

The Permission You've Been Waiting For

Before we dive into Olivia's journey, I need to give you permission for something that might feel uncomfortable at first:

You have permission to want more.

More money. More choices. More freedom. More security. More opportunity to practice nursing from a position of strength rather than desperation.

Wanting financial empowerment doesn't make you less caring. It doesn't make you greedy or selfish or "not nursey enough." In fact, I would argue that nurses who are financially stressed can't give their best to patients because they're distracted by survival concerns.

When you're worried about paying bills, part of your mental bandwidth is always occupied by financial stress. When you're working extra shifts just to make ends meet, you're more likely to make mistakes due to exhaustion. When you can't afford to leave a toxic workplace, you're forced to accept conditions that compromise both your well-being and patient care.

Financial empowerment makes caring sustainable.

You have permission to charge appropriately for your expertise. You have permission to negotiate for what you're worth. You have permission to create income streams from your nursing knowledge. You have permission to build wealth while serving others.

Most importantly, you have permission to prove that the best nurses aren't the ones who sacrifice everything—they're the ones who thrive and use that success to lift others.

Your Invitation to Transformation

Olivia's story begins with exhaustion and financial stress, but it doesn't end there. Over the next several chapters, you'll watch her discover possibilities she never knew existed. You'll see her transform from someone who feels powerless about money to someone who understands how to leverage her nursing expertise into lasting wealth.

But this isn't just Olivia's story—it's yours waiting to be written.

Every frustration Olivia experiences, you've probably felt. Every breakthrough she has, you can have too. Every strategy she learns, you can implement. Every limiting belief she overcomes, you can overcome.

The only difference between Olivia's story and your story is that you get to write the ending.

And here's something I want you to know: if this book resonates with you, if Olivia's story feels familiar, if you're ready to go deeper than what any book can provide—I've created something special for nurses who are serious about transformation.

The Nursing Wealthy Accelerator is where Olivia's journey becomes your reality through intensive coaching, accountability, and a community of nurses who refuse to accept financial limitations. But we're getting ahead of ourselves. First, let's see what Olivia discovers when she finally decides that "good enough" isn't good enough anymore.

Your Transformation Starts Now

So let's begin. Let's follow Olivia as she discovers what no one ever taught her in nursing school: that everything she's been told about nurses and money is wrong, and that she's been sitting on wealth-building superpowers all along.

Your transformation starts with her first step out of that hospital parking garage and into a completely different understanding of what's possible for nurses who refuse to accept financial limitations as the price of meaningful work.

The revolution starts with Olivia's story.

But it continues with yours.

Ready to discover what Olivia learns next? In Chapter 1, she'll uncover the hidden math behind her "good" salary and realize she's been trapped in a system designed to keep nurses financially dependent. But more importantly, she'll begin to see the first glimpse of another way forward.

UNLOCK YOUR BONUS RESOURCES

Scan to access your exclusive webinar on building financial freedom in nursing, plus downloadable tools and templates at

www.maryghazarian.com/nursingwealthy

01

PART I

FOUNDATION

CHAPTER 1

THE SALARY TRAP – WHY GOOD NURSES STAY POOR

"The biggest lie we've been told isn't that nurses don't make good money—it's that a steady paycheck equals financial success."

Olivia's Story

THREE WEEKS AFTER HER BREAKDOWN IN THE HOSPITAL PARKING garage, Olivia found herself sitting across from her friend Cara at their favorite coffee shop, surrounded by the weekend breakfast crowd. Cara had been her study partner through nursing school, her roommate during their first year as new grads, and now worked as a travel nurse making what seemed like incredible money.

"You look exhausted," Cara said, stirring her oat milk latte. "When's the last time you took a real day off?"

Olivia laughed bitterly. "Define 'real day off.' Yesterday I spent four hours meal prepping, did three loads of laundry, took Madison to soccer practice, and paid the water and gas bills. Does that count as rest?"

"I mean a day where you didn't think about work, money, or responsibilities. When you just... existed."

Olivia stared at her friend. The concept felt so foreign she couldn't even remember the last time that had happened. "Probably not since Madison was born. Maybe not since nursing school."

Cara leaned forward. "Olivia, you're one of the smartest nurses I know. You've been in the ICU for seven years, you have your bachelor's degree and an alphabet soup of certifications. You're practically running that unit some days. Why are you working yourself to death?"

"Because I need the money," Olivia said, as if it were obvious. "We've got the mortgage, Madison's daycare, the car payments. Mickey's construction work isn't always steady. I always wanted to be a stay at home mom, but right now I'm the stable income."

"But how much are you actually making per hour when you factor in all the extra time?"

Olivia frowned. "What do you mean? I make $34.50 an hour base pay, $51.75 for overtime."

Cara pulled out her phone and opened the calculator app. "Humor me. How many hours did you work last week?"

"Let's see... Monday and Tuesday were regular 12s, Wednesday I stayed late for a code that ran into the next shift, so that was 14 hours. Thursday off. Friday another 12, but I came in an hour early to help with short staffing. Saturday was supposed to be off, but they called me in for a double when Sarah called in sick. So... 54 hours total."

"And how much time did you spend on work-related stuff at home? Charting you couldn't finish, looking up medications, answering texts from your manager?"

Olivia thought about it. "Maybe... three hours total?"

"What about commute time?"

"Forty-five minutes each way, so... for five days, that's seven and a half hours."

Cara was scribbling furiously on a napkin. "Okay, so you worked 54 hours, plus 3 hours at home, plus 7.5 hours commuting. That's 64.5 hours total related to work. Now, what did you actually take home after taxes, parking, union dues, all of that?"

Olivia pulled up her banking app. "My deposit was $1,847 for the week."

Cara divided the numbers on her phone's calculator. "$1,847 divided by 64.5 hours... Olivia, you made $28.63 an hour."

Olivia stared at the phone screen. "That can't be right."

"It gets worse. What about all the money you spend because you're exhausted from working so much? The takeout because you're too tired to cook, the coffee shop runs, the convenience purchases?"

Olivia's stomach dropped. She thought about the week Cara was describing. Three dinner deliveries when she was too exhausted to cook after her shifts. Two $6 coffee drinks from the hospital café seeing as the break room coffee was terrible. A $40 grocery pickup order that included mostly pre-made foods as she didn't have time to meal prep. Gas for the extra trips when she forgot things due to exhaustion.

"Maybe... $150 extra that week?"

Cara nodded grimly. "So really, you netted $1,697 for 64.5 hours of work-related time. That's $26.31 an hour."

"Oof." Olivia felt like she'd been punched in the stomach. "But... that's barely more than minimum wage in some places."

"For someone with a bachelor's degree, seven years of experience, and advanced certifications who literally saves lives," Cara said softly.

The coffee shop suddenly felt too loud, too bright. Olivia watched a young woman at the next table working on her laptop, looking relaxed and focused. She wondered what that woman did for work, whether she made more than $26 an hour, whether she had to worry about being called in on her days off.

"How is this possible?" Olivia whispered. "I'm supposed to have a good job. Everyone says nurses make decent money."

Cara's expression was gentle but serious. "Because the system is designed to keep you thinking you're doing well while actually keeping you trapped. You make just enough to afford the lifestyle they want you to have—the house payment that keeps you tied to steady work, the car payment that requires reliable income, the daycare costs that make leaving impossible."

"But you're a nurse too, and you seem to be doing fine financially."

Cara smiled. "I am now. But it took me three years to figure out what you're starting to see today. Our traditional nursing jobs aren't designed to make us wealthy, Olivia. They're designed to make you stable enough to keep showing up, but not prosperous enough to have real choices."

Olivia thought about her weekly routine: the alarm at 5:30 AM, the rushed breakfast, the commute spent mentally preparing for whatever crisis awaited. The twelve hours of non-stop patient care, critical decisions, life-and-death moments. The drive home in traffic, too tired to think clearly. The evening spent recovering just enough to do it again.

"So what's the answer?" she asked. "Quit nursing? I can't do that. This is all I know, and we need the income."

"The answer isn't quitting nursing," Cara said. "The answer is understanding that your nursing skills are worth way more than what your employer is paying you for them. You just need to learn how to capture that value."

"How much do you think this pen is worth?" Cara asked, picking up a cheap ballpoint she had been using.

"I don't know, maybe twenty-five cents?"

"Right. Now, the fancy jewelry store across the street sells a sterling silver ballpoint pen for $250. Same exact function—both put ink on paper. But one comes in a little blue box with their name on it, and suddenly people will pay a thousand times more for it."

She took the plastic blue cap off the pen. "The difference isn't what it does. The difference is how it's positioned, where it's sold, and what story comes with it. Your nursing skills are the same way. You're selling them like this twenty-five-cent pen when you could be positioning them like the silver one."

Cara reached into her bag and pulled out a small notebook. "Can I show you something?" She opened to a page filled with numbers. "This is what I made last month as a travel nurse: $12,000 gross, about $9,500 take-home after taxes and expenses."

Olivia's eyes widened. "In one month?"

"In one month. Same nursing skills you have, same license, same responsibilities. The only difference is I learned how to position myself as a specialist rather than just another staff nurse. I learned how to negotiate contracts, how to maximize my tax benefits, and how to make my money work for me instead of just trading time for dollars."

Cara continued, "But travel nursing isn't the only way. There are nurses making six figures in telemedicine, others building consulting businesses around their expertise, some creating online courses that generate passive income. The problem isn't that nursing doesn't pay well—it's that employed nursing has artificial limits."

Confused, Olivia blurted. "But I have Madison, and Mickey's work is here. I can't just travel around the country."

"You don't have to. There are dozens of ways to leverage your ICU expertise without leaving town. The key is understanding that your knowledge, your skills, your experience—they're assets that can generate income beyond just trading your time for an hourly wage."

Cara closed her notebook and leaned back. "Olivia, what if I told you that this time next year, you could be working fewer hours and making more money? What if you could have Saturdays off to take Madison to the park instead of covering for call-ins? What if you could pay off your debt and start actually building wealth instead of just surviving paycheck to paycheck?"

"I'd say it sounds too good to be true."

"It would have sounded that way to me three years ago too. Honestly, the nurses who are financially successful aren't necessarily smarter or more talented than you. They just learned to see their worth differently and position themselves accordingly."

Olivia stared out the coffee shop window, watching people walk by with their weekend plans and relaxed expressions. She allowed herself to imagine what it would feel like to be one of them—to have choices, to have breathing room, to work because she wanted to contribute rather than because she desperately needed every paycheck.

"Where do I start?" she asked quietly.

Cara smiled. "First, you have to stop thinking like an employee and start thinking like a professional who happens to be employed. Then, you need to understand exactly how much you're really worth—not just what your employer is willing to pay you."

As they left the coffee shop that morning, Olivia was quietly hopeful. She knew that next month's bills wouldn't somehow be easier to pay, but she started seeing a different path forward.

The salary trap she'd been caught in wasn't permanent. It was just the first cage she needed to learn how to unlock.

The Hidden Math Behind Your "Good" Salary

Cara's calculation with Olivia isn't unusual—it's the norm for nurses caught in what I call the "salary illusion." This is the dangerous belief that a steady paycheck with benefits equals financial success, even when the math tells a completely different story.

```
┌─────────────────────────────┐
│      SHIFT RECEIPT          │
├─────────────────────────────┤
│ RATE $40/hr × 8h    $320    │
├─────────────────────────────┤
│ LESS TAXES          −$80    │
├─────────────────────────────┤
│ OUT-OF-POCKET       $15     │
│ PARKING             $15     │
│ LUNCH               $10     │
├─────────────────────────────┤
│ TIME ADD-ONS        1h      │
│ COMMUTE             0.5h    │
│ CHARTING            0.5h    │
├─────────────────────────────┤
│ TRUE HOURLY    $22,63/h     │
│                             │
│               Nursing       │
│               Wealthy       │
└─────────────────────────────┘
```

Let me share the framework I use with coaching clients to calculate their true hourly wage, because once you see these numbers clearly, you can't unsee them. And that clarity becomes the motivation you need to make different choices.

The Real Cost Calculation

Most nurses drastically underestimate the hidden costs of their employment. Here's how to calculate what you're actually earning:

Step 1: Calculate Your True Hours

- Scheduled work hours
- Overtime and extra shifts
- Unpaid time (arriving early, staying late, completing charting at home)
- Commute time
- Work-related activities (mandatory meetings, continuing education on your own time)

Step 2: Calculate Your Real Costs

- Parking fees (often $200-400 monthly)
- Professional expenses (uniforms, shoes, certification renewals, continuing education)
- Transportation costs (gas, vehicle wear from shift work schedules)
- Convenience costs (eating out due to exhaustion, expensive coffee, last-minute purchases)
- Healthcare costs related to work stress and physical demands

Step 3: Calculate Your Net Take-Home

- Gross pay minus taxes
- Minus benefits deductions
- Minus professional expenses
- Minus work-related convenience costs

Step 4: Divide Net Income by True Hours

When I walk nurses through this calculation, the results are consistently shocking. Experienced ICU nurses like Olivia often discover they're earning $25-30 per hour in real terms, despite base pay rates of $35-40 per hour.

The Overtime Trap

The most insidious part of the salary trap is how overtime is presented as an opportunity to "make extra money" when it's actually a wealth-destruction mechanism disguised as a benefit.

Here's why overtime keeps you poor:

- **The Tax Penalty:** Overtime puts you in higher tax brackets, meaning you keep less of each overtime dollar than regular hours.
- **The Exhaustion Cost:** Working extra shifts leads to poor financial decisions due to fatigue—expensive convenience purchases, impulse buying, failure to meal prep or budget properly.
- **The Opportunity Cost:** Time spent on overtime could be invested in activities that build long-term wealth—education, networking, developing additional income streams.
- **The Health Cost:** Overtime creates physical and mental stress that leads to medical expenses and reduced career longevity.

When you factor in these hidden costs, overtime often generates less than $15 per hour in real value while stealing the time and energy you need to build actual wealth.

Why the System Keeps You Financially Dependent

The nursing salary structure isn't accidental—it's carefully designed to maintain a workforce that's financially dependent and therefore unable to leave or negotiate from positions of strength.

Here's how healthcare organizations ensure you stay trapped:

- **Golden Handcuffs Benefits:** Health insurance, retirement matching, and paid time off that's expensive to replace but keeps you tied to steady employment.
- **The Lifestyle Inflation Pipeline:** Regular small raises that feel meaningful but barely keep pace with inflation, designed to increase your lifestyle expenses without building real wealth.

- **Shift Differential Illusions:** Night and weekend premiums that seem substantial but often amount to $2-4 per hour—not enough to justify the health and social costs.
- **Overtime Availability:** The constant option to work extra shifts creates the illusion that you control your income, when actually you're just trading more time for slightly more money.

The most brilliant aspect of this system is that it makes you feel grateful. "At least I have job security." "At least I have benefits." "At least I can pick up overtime when I need extra money."

Meanwhile, healthcare systems generate enormous profits while keeping their largest expense category—nursing labor—artificially constrained.

The Professional Devaluation Problem

Beyond the financial mechanics, the salary trap perpetuates a more subtle but equally damaging problem: the systematic devaluation of nursing expertise.

When you're paid an hourly wage like an entry-level worker despite having advanced education, specialized skills, and life-or-death responsibilities, it sends a message about your worth. Over time, many nurses internalize this message and begin to undervalue their own expertise.

I see this constantly in coaching clients who hesitate to charge appropriate rates for consulting work, who underestimate the value of their knowledge, who apologize for asking for fair compensation. The salary trap doesn't just limit your income—it limits your sense of professional worth.

The Compound Effect of Financial Stress

The real tragedy of the salary trap isn't just the immediate financial limitation—it's how financial stress compounds to limit every other aspect of your life and career.

When you're worried about money:

- You can't take career risks that might lead to advancement
- You can't invest time in education or professional development
- You can't leave toxic work environments
- You can't be selective about assignments or employers
- You can't advocate boldly for patients or colleagues

Financial stress doesn't just affect your bank account—it affects your ability to be the nurse you're capable of being.

Breaking Free: The Mindset Shift

The first step out of the salary trap is recognizing that your current financial situation isn't a reflection of your worth or abilities—it's a reflection of a system designed to keep you financially constrained.

The second step is understanding that your nursing expertise has market value far beyond what your employer is willing to pay for it. The skills that make you a great ICU nurse—crisis management, quick decision-making, patient advocacy, complex problem-solving—are exactly the skills that create wealth in other contexts.

The third step is recognizing that you have more control over your financial situation than you've been led to believe. The same competence you bring to patient care can be applied to managing your money, building additional income streams, and creating the financial security you deserve.

Like Olivia, you might be sitting on a goldmine of valuable expertise while feeling financially trapped. The trap is real, but it's not permanent. Every nurse who's achieved financial independence started exactly where you are right now—aware that something isn't working but not yet sure what to do about it.

The difference between nurses who stay trapped and nurses who build wealth isn't talent, luck, or circumstances. It's understanding how the system works and choosing to play by different rules.

In the next chapter, we'll follow Olivia as she begins to examine the money beliefs that have kept her accepting less than she's worth, and discovers how to rewrite the story she's been telling herself about what's possible for nurses like her.

Wealth Work: Calculate Your True Hourly Wage

Time needed: 30 minutes

Impact: High - This exercise often provides the "wake-up call" moment that motivates real change

Step 1: Track Your Real Hours (1 week)

For one week, track every minute related to your work:

- Clock-in to clock-out time
- Commute time each day
- Time spent on work activities at home
- Time spent reading work emails, texts, or calls on off days
- Time spent on mandatory education or meetings

Total work-related hours this week: _____

Step 2: Calculate Your Real Costs (1 month)

Add up all work-related expenses for one month:

- Parking fees
- Gas and vehicle wear
- Work clothing and shoes
- Professional fees (licenses, certifications)
- Convenience costs (coffee, meals out due to exhaustion)
- Any other expenses you incur because you work

Total monthly work-related costs: $ _____

Step 3: Calculate Your Net Income

- Gross monthly pay: $ _____
- Minus taxes and deductions: $ _____
- Minus work-related costs: $ _____
- **Net monthly income:** $ _____

Step 4: Calculate Your True Hourly Rate

- Net monthly income ÷ total monthly work hours = Your real hourly wage
- **My true hourly wage:** $ _____

Step 5: Reflection Questions

1. How does your true hourly wage compare to what you thought you were making?
2. How does it compare to other jobs that require similar education and responsibility?
3. What emotions come up when you see this number?
4. If you shared this calculation with someone outside healthcare, what do you think their reaction would be?
5. What would have to change for you to feel appropriately compensated for your expertise?

Step 6: The Possibility Question

If you discovered you could make the same amount of money working 20% fewer hours, what would you do with that extra time?

Write your answer in detail. This becomes your motivation for the changes ahead.

Coming Next: In Chapter 2, Olivia discovers that her financial struggles aren't a personal failing—they're the result of money beliefs she inherited from a system designed to keep nurses financially dependent. She'll learn how to identify and rewrite the stories that have been limiting her potential, and you'll discover how to do the same.

REWRITING YOUR MONEY STORY

"Your current financial situation isn't the result of your nursing salary—it's the result of the money story you've been telling yourself since childhood."

Olivia's Story

TWO DAYS AFTER HER COFFEE SHOP REVELATION WITH CARA, Olivia found herself lying awake at 3 AM, staring at the ceiling while Mickey slept peacefully beside her. Her mind was racing, cycling through numbers, possibilities, and a growing sense that everything she thought she knew about money and nursing might be wrong.

She slipped out of bed and padded to the kitchen, making herself a cup of tea and settling at the small table where she paid bills each month. In the quiet darkness, surrounded by the weight of monthly statements and budget spreadsheets, she tried to make sense of what Cara had shown her.

$26.31 an hour. The number felt insulting every time it surfaced in her mind. How had she convinced herself that she was doing well financially when the math told such a different story?

She opened her laptop and pulled up a document she'd never thought to create before: a list of every financial belief she'd grown up with. The exercise felt strange, almost therapeutic, like excavating layers of her own psyche she'd never examined.

Money doesn't grow on trees. Her mother's voice echoed in her memory, always said with a tone of gentle but firm limitation whenever Olivia had asked for something as a child.

We're not the kind of people who have money. This one came from her father, usually delivered with a shrug that suggested resignation to circumstances beyond their control. She recalled her father collecting cans and bottles from recycling bins every Tuesday morning in her childhood to return at 5 cents a piece.

Rich people are lucky or they inherited it. Her parents again, spoken while watching the news or driving through affluent neighborhoods. Once or twice she recalled they had taken a special drive down mansion row to marvel at the houses several times the size of her own childhood home. Homes other people lived in, but that were out of reach for her and her family.

Nurses don't go into it for the money. This had come from her nursing school professors, her clinical instructors, even her current colleagues. It was always said with pride, as if financial motivation somehow tainted the nobility of the profession.

Be grateful for what you have. The universal family motto, applied to everything from Christmas gifts to career opportunities.

As she typed, Olivia realized these were the silent operating system that had been running her financial life for thirty-two years. Every decision about money, every career choice, every moment when she'd accepted less than she deserved, could be traced back to these deeply embedded beliefs.

She thought about nursing school, when she'd chosen the local option over the option that had better clinical rotations because "we can't afford the expensive school." She'd never even looked into scholarships or financial aid options. The assumption that money was out of reach had been automatic.

She remembered her first job offer, when she'd accepted the salary without negotiation because "they're offering me good money, and I should be grateful." She'd never researched market rates or considered that negotiation was even possible.

She thought about last year, when a Nurse Practitioner friend had mentioned she was making $95,000 annually in a clinic role. Olivia's immediate reaction had been, "Must be nice," followed by a mental explanation of why that level of income wasn't realistic for someone like her. She'd never investigated what it would take to become a Nurse Practitioner or whether it might be worth the investment.

The pattern was becoming clear: at every decision point, she'd chosen limitation over possibility, security over growth, gratitude over ambition. She wasn't lazy or unworthy. But, her money story told her that anything more wasn't meant for people like her.

Her phone buzzed with a text message. Cara: *Hey! Can't sleep either? I've been thinking about our conversation. Want to grab breakfast before your shift tomorrow?*

Olivia smiled and typed back: *Yes. I think I'm ready to hear what you learned about changing your money story.*

The next morning at the same coffee shop, Cara arrived with a worn notebook and an expression that suggested she'd been waiting for this conversation for a long time.

"So," Cara said, settling into her chair, "tell me what's been going through your mind since yesterday."

Olivia shared her 3 AM revelation about the beliefs that had been shaping her financial choices. Cara listened intently, nodding at recognizable threads.

"I went through the exact same process three years ago," Cara said when Olivia finished. "I realized I'd been making financial decisions based on stories I'd inherited from my childhood, not on my current reality as a skilled professional."

She opened her notebook to a page titled "Old Money Story vs. New Money Story."

"Look, here's what I used to believe about myself and money:" Cara read from the left side of the page. "*I come from a working-class family, so I should be grateful for any steady job. Wanting more money is greedy. Rich people are different from me. I don't know enough about money to make good decisions. Nursing is a calling, not a business.*"

Olivia felt a jolt of recognition. "Those could be my exact thoughts."

"Now look at what I chose to believe instead:" Cara moved to the right side of the page. "*I come from a family that values hard work, which serves me well in building wealth. Money is a tool that allows me to serve others more effectively. Wealthy people often started where I am now. I can learn about money the same way I learned about nursing. Nursing is both a calling and a valuable profession that deserves appropriate compensation.*"

Cara looked up from her notebook. "The facts of my background didn't change. But I changed the story I told myself about what those facts meant for my future."

"How do you just... decide to believe different things?" Olivia asked. "Some of these beliefs feel like facts."

Cara laughed. "They felt like facts to me too. But here's what I learned: most of our money beliefs aren't based on facts—they're based on other people's interpretations of their circumstances, usually from decades ago."

She leaned forward. "Think about it. Your parents' financial situation when you

Rewriting Your Money Story

Old Story	New Story
Nurses don't go into it for the money	Nurses deserve appropriate compensation
Talking about money is unprofessional	Talking about money is empowering
Good nurses are selfless	Good nurses value themselves

Nursing Wealthy

were growing up—was that based on their education level, the economy at the time, their career choices, their knowledge about money?"

"All of those things, I guess."

"Right. So their beliefs about money made sense for their situation. But you're not in their situation. You have a professional degree, specialized skills, and opportunities they never had. Why would their limitations apply to you?"

Olivia felt a loosening of the constraints she'd carried for so long they felt like a second skin. "I never thought about it that way."

Cara continued, "The same thing happened with the messaging I got in nursing school. All that talk about 'not being in it for the money'— that came from nursing educators who were often underpaid themselves, working in a system that had taught them to accept less. They passed on their limitations as if they were virtues."

"But what if wanting more money does make me less... nursey?" Olivia asked, voicing a fear she'd never spoken aloud.

"Olivia, think about the last time you were really stressed about money. How present were you with your patients that day? How much mental energy did you have for clinical reasoning when part of your brain was calculating whether you could afford Madison's school supplies?"

Olivia remembered last month, when she'd been so distracted by an unexpected car repair bill that she'd almost missed a subtle change in her patient's respiratory status. The financial stress had actually made her a less attentive nurse.

"Financial security doesn't make you less caring," Cara continued. "It makes caring sustainable. When you're not worried about survival, you can focus completely on service."

Cara flipped to another page in her notebook. "Here's another exercise that helped me. I want you to close your eyes and imagine two versions of yourself."

"Version One: You continue on your current path. Five years from now, you're still picking up overtime to make ends meet, still stressed about money, still feeling trapped by your circumstances. How does that nurse show up for her patients? How does she feel about her career? What kind of energy does she bring to her family?"

Feeling a bit silly, Olivia closed her eyes. She pictured herself at thirty-seven, even more exhausted than she was now, possibly dealing with the physical toll of years of financial stress and overwork. She shrunk in her chair. The image was depressing.

"Version Two: You learn to value your expertise appropriately and build financial security. Five years from now, you work because you choose to, not because you have to. You can advocate boldly for your patients when you're not afraid of losing your job. You can be fully present no longer distracted by money worries. You're an example to other nurses of what's possible. How does that nurse show up?"

This version of herself stood taller, spoke with more confidence, had energy left over after work to truly engage with Madison and Mickey. She could take career risks, pursue additional education, maybe even mentor other nurses who were where she used to be.

"That's the nurse I want to be," Olivia said quietly.

"Then that's the money story you need to write," Cara replied. "Not one based on your parents' limitations or nursing school's outdated messaging, but one based on who you are now and who you want to become."

Cara tore a sheet out of her notebook and slid the blank piece of paper across the table along with a pen. "Try this. Write a new money story that honors your nursing values while supporting your financial goals. What would you tell Madison about money and work and worth? What story would serve her better than the one you inherited?"

Olivia picked up the pen and began to write:

> *I am a skilled healthcare professional with valuable expertise.*
> *My ability to manage crisis situations, make quick decisions*
> *under pressure, and care for people during their most vulnerable*
> *moments represents years of education and training. This*

expertise has significant value, and I deserve to be compensated appropriately for it.

Money is a tool that allows me to serve others more effectively. When I'm financially secure, I can focus completely on patient care instead of worrying about bills. I can make career decisions based on where I can have the most impact, not where I can barely survive.

Building wealth doesn't make me less caring—it makes me more capable of caring sustainably for the long term. Every dollar I earn through my nursing expertise enables me to continue serving others while also providing security for my family.

I can learn about money and investing the same way I learned about pathophysiology and pharmacology. Financial knowledge is a skill I can develop, not a mysterious talent I either have or don't have.

The same qualities that make me a good nurse—attention to detail, the ability to assess and adapt, persistence in the face of challenges—make me capable of building wealth.

As she wrote, Olivia felt excitement about her future. A genuine anticipation for what she might create.

"How does that feel?" Cara asked when Olivia finished reading her new story aloud.

"Scary," Olivia admitted. "But also... possible. Like maybe I've been limiting myself for no good reason."

Cara smiled. "That's exactly how it should feel. Your new money story should stretch you just beyond your current comfort zone. It should make you a little nervous because it's calling you to become more than you've been before."

Cara had one last exercise for Olivia. "Before you tuck that paper away, I want you to write a number on the back of the paper. The number that you feel it would take to feel financial freedom."

Olivia scribbled zero after zero on the paper. She had never thought about income and savings beyond her yearly five-figure earnings. She settled on a seven figure number and tucked the paper into a zippered pocket in her purse.

As they left the coffee shop that morning, Olivia felt like she was carrying a different future in her bag along with her work badge and stethoscope. The same shift awaited her at Metropolis General, the same patients, the same responsibilities. But she was approaching it all with a fundamentally different understanding of her own worth.

The story she'd been telling herself about money and nursing wasn't the truth—it was just one possible interpretation of her circumstances. And if she could choose to believe a limiting story, she could just as easily choose to believe an empowering one.

The only question now was: what would she do with this new story?

The Money Stories That Shape Us

Cara's conversation with Olivia reveals something I see consistently in my coaching practice: most nurses' financial struggles aren't caused by their circumstances—they're caused by the stories they've inherited about money, worth, and what's possible for people like them.

These stories operate below conscious awareness, influencing hundreds of small decisions that keep talented professionals trapped in financial mediocrity. The good news is that once you recognize these stories for what they are—inherited beliefs rather than absolute truths—you can choose to rewrite them.

Where Money Stories Come From

Our financial beliefs are formed early and reinforced constantly through family messages, cultural conditioning, and professional socialization.

For nurses, this creates a particularly toxic combination of inherited limitation and professional guilt about financial motivation.

Family Money Messages: Most nurses grew up in working-class or middle-class families where financial security was valued over wealth building. Common themes include:

- "Money doesn't grow on trees" (scarcity mindset)
- "We're not the kind of people who have money" (identity limitation)
- "Rich people are different from us" (othering of financial success)
- "Be grateful for what you have" (acceptance of limitation)

These messages often came from parents who were genuinely doing their best with limited resources and knowledge. The problem isn't that these beliefs were wrong for their circumstances—it's that we unconsciously carry them into completely different circumstances where they no longer serve us.

Professional Conditioning: Nursing education and culture add another layer of limiting beliefs specifically about the incompatibility of caring and earning:

- "Nurses don't go into it for the money" (financial motivation as impure)
- "It's a calling, not a job" (spiritual work shouldn't be well-compensated)
- "Patient care comes first" (personal needs, including financial needs, are secondary)
- "We're in it to serve others" (self-service, including building wealth, is selfish)

This professional conditioning is particularly insidious considering that it wraps financial limitation in moral language, making it feel virtuous to accept less than you're worth.

How Money Stories Sabotage Success

These inherited beliefs don't just affect how you think about money—they affect every financial decision you make, usually without you realizing it.

Career Choices: Nurses with limiting money stories consistently choose security over growth, stability over opportunity. They accept the first job offer without negotiation, stay in positions longer than serves them, and avoid career risks that could lead to advancement.

Salary Negotiations: The belief that you should be "grateful for what you have" makes salary negotiation feel greedy or ungrateful. Many nurses have never negotiated as it feels incompatible with their professional identity.

Investment Decisions: Stories about not being "money people" lead to avoidance of financial planning and investing. Nurses often keep money in low-yield savings accounts for years because investing feels too risky or complicated for "people like them."

Business Opportunities: The strongest limiting beliefs emerge around entrepreneurship. Nurses with restrictive money stories can't imagine charging for their expertise stemming from a feeling of unease about commercializing their caring nature.

The Professional Identity Trap

One of the most challenging aspects of rewriting money stories as a nurse is that our professional identity has become entangled with financial limitation. We've been taught that caring and earning are inversely related—that the more you care about money, the less you must care about patients.

This creates what I call the "professional identity trap"—the fear that financial success will somehow compromise your identity as a nurse or make you less authentic in your caring.

The truth is exactly the opposite. Nurses who are financially stressed are less present with patients, more likely to make errors due to distraction, and more prone to burnout. Financial security enhances your ability to care by removing survival concerns that compete with patient focus.

Rewriting Your Money Story: A Framework

The process of changing your money story isn't about positive thinking or affirmations—it's about examining your inherited beliefs logically and choosing ones that serve your current goals and circumstances.

Step 1: Identify Your Current Story Write down every belief you have about money, wealth, and financial success. Include beliefs about your worthiness, your capabilities, and what's possible for "people like you." Don't edit or judge—just capture what you actually believe.

Step 2: Trace the Origins For each belief, ask: Where did this come from? Whose voice do I hear when I think this? What circumstances was this belief originally based on?

Step 3: Evaluate Current Relevance Ask: Is this belief based on my current circumstances or outdated information? Does this belief serve my current goals? What opportunities have I missed because of this belief?

Step 4: Choose Empowering Alternatives For each limiting belief, craft an alternative that:

- Acknowledges your nursing values
- Supports your financial goals
- Feels challenging but achievable
- Honors your professional identity while expanding your possibilities

Step 5: Test and Refine Begin making decisions based on your new story. Notice what feels authentic versus what triggers old programming. Refine your new beliefs based on what you learn through action.

Common Money Story Transformations for Nurses

Here are the most powerful belief shifts I see in successful nursing clients:

From: "Nurses don't go into it for the money"
To: "Nurses deserve appropriate compensation for life-saving expertise"

From: "Money isn't important if you love what you do"
To: "Financial security allows me to love what I do sustainably"

From: "I should be grateful for what I have"
To: "Gratitude and ambition can coexist"

From: "Rich people are different from me"
To: "Wealthy people often started where I am now"

From: "I'm not good with money"
To: "I can learn about money the same way I learned about nursing"

From: "Wanting more is selfish"
To: "Building wealth enables me to serve others more effectively"

The Values Integration Challenge

The most successful money story rewrites don't abandon nursing values—they integrate financial goals with caring motivations. This integration is crucial as any new story that feels incompatible with your core identity will eventually be rejected by your subconscious.

Effective new money stories for nurses often include themes like:

- Financial security enhances rather than diminishes your ability to care
- Building wealth creates opportunities to serve others at a larger scale
- Professional expertise deserves professional compensation
- Taking care of yourself financially is part of taking care of others sustainably

The Ripple Effect

When you successfully rewrite your money story, the effects extend far beyond your bank account. You begin showing up differently in all areas of your life—more confident in your worth, more willing to advocate for yourself and others, more present given that you're not constantly worried about survival.

Perhaps most importantly, you become a living example to other nurses of what's possible when you refuse to accept financial limitation as the price of meaningful work. Your transformation gives others permission to examine their own limiting beliefs and consider what might be possible for them.

Your new money story becomes a gift you give not just to yourself and your family, but to the entire nursing profession.

Wealth Work: Rewrite Your Money Story

Time needed: 45 minutes

Impact: Foundational - This exercise addresses the root beliefs that drive all financial behavior

Part 1: Excavate Your Current Story (15 minutes)

Complete these sentences with your immediate, uncensored responses:

About Money:

- Money is _____
- Rich people are _____
- I can't afford to _____ because _____
- My family always said money _____

About Your Worth:

- I deserve _____

- People like me don't _____

- I'm not the type of person who _____

- I should be grateful for _____ and not ask for more

About Nursing and Money:

- Good nurses _____

- Wanting money as a nurse means _____

- I became a nurse to _____, not to _____

- If I focus on money, I might _____

Part 2: Trace the Origins (10 minutes)

For each belief above, ask:

- Whose voice do I hear when I think this?
- What circumstances was this belief based on?
- How old was I when I first learned this?
- What did this belief protect me from or help me achieve then?

Part 3: Evaluate Current Relevance (10 minutes)

For each belief, consider:

- Is this still true for my current circumstances?
- Does this belief serve my current goals?
- What opportunities have I missed because of this belief?
- How has this belief affected my financial decisions?

Part 4: Craft Your New Story (10 minutes)

Write a 2-3 paragraph "New Money Story" that:

- Honors your nursing values and caring nature
- Positions money as a tool for greater service
- Acknowledges your professional expertise and worth
- Feels challenging but authentic to who you want to become

My New Money Story:

[Write your story here, focusing on integration of your caring values with financial empowerment]

_____

_____

_____

_____

_____

_____

_____

_____

_____

_____

_____

_____

_____

_____

_____

_____

Part 5: Integration Questions

1. What would change about your daily decisions if you fully believed your new story?
2. What would you do differently in your career if you operated from these new beliefs?
3. What financial opportunity would you pursue first if you truly believed you deserved financial success?
4. How would believing your new story affect how you show up for your patients?
5. What would you want to teach your children (or future children) about money and worth based on your new story?

Part 6: Implementation Commitment

Choose one small action you'll take this week that aligns with your new money story rather than your old beliefs. This could be:

- Researching salary ranges for your position
- Having a conversation about your career goals
- Opening an investment account
- Calculating your true hourly wage and sharing it with someone you trust

Saying "no" to an overtime shift to protect your energy for wealth-building activities

My commitment: This week I will _____

Coming Next: In Chapter 3, Olivia discovers that she's been calculating her worth all wrong and learns about the hidden assets that every nurse possesses—assets that traditional financial planning completely ignores. She'll calculate her true net worth and realize she's not starting from zero; she's starting from a position of strength she never knew she had.

02

PART II

THE WEALTH FRAMEWORK

W - WEALTH MINDSET & WHOLE NET WORTH

"Traditional net worth calculations miss the most valuable assets nurses possess. You're not starting from zero—you're starting with intangible assets."

Olivia's Story

OLIVIA STARED AT THE EMAIL IN HER INBOX, READING IT FOR THE third time in disbelief. The subject line was simple: "Investment Consultation - Complimentary Session." It had arrived two days after her conversation with Cara about money stories, almost as if the universe was testing her commitment to thinking differently about her financial future.

The email was from a financial advisor Mickey's coworker had recommended, offering a free initial consultation to "assess your current financial position and discuss wealth-building strategies." Three weeks ago, Olivia would have deleted it immediately. The idea of sitting across from a financial professional and admitting how little she had saved felt mortifying.

But her new money story was still fresh in her mind: *I can learn about money the same way I learned about nursing. I deserve to understand my options.*

She scheduled the appointment for her next day off.

Now she sat in Don Beadle's polished office, surrounded by mahogany furniture and diplomas that radiated financial competence. Don himself was younger than she'd expected, probably early forties, with the kind of calm confidence that came from helping people solve problems all day.

"So, Olivia," Don said, settling behind his desk with a yellow legal pad. "Tell me about your current financial situation. What assets do you have?"

Olivia felt her stomach drop. This was the moment she'd been dreading. "Well, we have about $3,200 in our checking account, maybe $800 in savings. Mickey has a small pension from his previous job, probably around $15,000. I have about $8,000 in my hospital's retirement plan."

Don nodded politely while writing, his expression neutral. "Any other investments? Real estate besides your primary residence? Business interests?"

"No, nothing like that." Olivia felt heat rising in her cheeks. "We own our house, but we only bought it three years ago, so there's not much equity. Maybe $20,000?"

"Okay, and what about debt?"

This part was even worse. "We owe about $585,000 on the mortgage, $18,000 on my student loans, $4,200 on credit cards, and $12,000 on Mickey's truck."

Don calculated quietly. When he looked up, his expression was professional but not particularly encouraging. "So your traditional net worth is approximately $-252,200. That's your assets minus your liabilities."

Olivia felt deflated. A networth six figures in the negative. After seven years of working as a nurse, after all the overtime shifts and sacrifices and careful budgeting, she was worth less than her morning coffee.

"I have to be honest, Olivia," Don continued, his tone gentle but matter-of-fact. "For someone your age with your income level, this is... concerning. While the house is good debt as it's an appreciating asset, you're significantly behind where you should be for retirement planning.

We really need to focus on dramatically increasing your savings rate and getting you into some aggressive growth investments."

She shrunk. *Significantly behind. Concerning.* She'd known she wasn't wealthy, but hearing it quantified by a professional made her feel like she'd failed at adulting entirely.

"What should I have at my age?" she asked quietly.

"Financial planners generally recommend having one year's salary saved by age 30, three years' salary by 40. At 32, earning roughly $70,000 annually, you should ideally have around $140,000 in assets."

Olivia did the math quickly. She was way behind where she "should" be. The gap felt insurmountable.

Don was pulling out glossy brochures and starting to discuss investment options, but Olivia wasn't really listening. Her mind was spinning with shame and confusion. How had she gotten so far behind? She'd worked constantly, lived modestly, and made responsible choices. Where had all the money gone?

"I think I need some time to process this," she said, interrupting Don mid-sentence about index funds and risk tolerance.

"Of course. But Olivia, the important thing is that you're starting now. Time is your most valuable asset for building wealth. The sooner we get you on an aggressive savings plan—"

"Thank you," Olivia said, standing abruptly. "I'll call you."

She made it to her car before the tears started. Sitting in the parking lot of Don's office building, she felt more hopeless about money than she had before Cara's wake-up call. At least when she was in denial about her money, she'd had the illusion that she was doing okay. Now she knew she was both underpaid and behind on savings. The hole felt too deep to ever climb out of.

Her phone buzzed. A text from Cara: *How did the financial advisor go?*

Instead of texting back, Olivia called. Cara answered on the first ring.

"He said I'm significantly behind where I should be," Olivia said without preamble, her voice thick with tears. "My net worth is on life-support. I feel pathetic."

"Whoa, slow down. Where are you right now?"

"In the parking lot outside his office."

"Stay right there. I'm coming to get you."

Thirty minutes later, Cara slid into the passenger seat of Olivia's car carrying two coffee cups and wearing an expression that was half-sympathy, half-amusement.

"Okay, first things first," Cara said, handing Olivia a latte. "Traditional financial advisors are trained to calculate net worth using a very specific formula that completely ignores the most valuable assets that nurses possess."

"What do you mean?"

Cara pulled out her phone and opened the notes app. "Let's do this properly. Don calculated your traditional net worth—your financial assets minus your debts. But he completely ignored your professional assets, your expertise, your network, and your earning potential."

She started typing. "Your nursing license. What's that worth?"

"I don't know. I paid maybe $200 to get it?"

Cara laughed. "Olivia, your nursing license gives you access to employment in every single state in the country, plus most developed countries internationally. It's recession-proof income that will be in demand for the rest of your working life. Conservative estimate: $500,000 in lifetime earning power compared to jobs that don't require professional licensing."

Olivia blinked. She'd never thought of her license as a financial asset.

"Your ICU expertise," Cara continued. "You've spent seven years learning to manage the most critical patients in the hospital. You can work anywhere, anytime, at premium rates. During COVID, travel ICU nurses were making $5,000-8,000 per week. Your specialty knowledge has serious market value."

Cara was typing rapidly. "Your professional network. How many nurses do you know? How many doctors? Nurse managers? Administrators?"

"I don't know... maybe 200 people across all the places I've worked?"

"Each of those relationships represents potential opportunities—job referrals, consulting work, partnership possibilities. Conservative value: $200,000."

"This seems like you're making up numbers," Olivia protested.

"Am I? When Dr. Peters needed someone to help train staff on the new ECMO protocol last month, who did he ask?"

"Me."

"And when Sarah was looking for someone to cover her vacation shifts, who did she text first?"

"Me."

"And when your old manager from the step-down unit heard about an opening in the cardiac surgery ICU, who did she call?"

"Me." Olivia was starting to see the pattern.

Cara nodded. "Your reputation, your relationships, your expertise—these things have real economic value. They create opportunities that generate income. But traditional financial planning completely ignores them."

She showed Olivia the notes on her phone:

Olivia's Traditional Net Worth: Flatlined

Olivia's Professional Assets:
- Nursing license and credentials: $500,000
- ICU expertise and specialization: $300,000
- Professional network and reputation: $200,000
- Crisis-proof income stability: $600,000

Olivia's True Net Worth: $1,647,800

Olivia stared at the screen. "This can't be right."

"Why not? You have skills that took years to develop and can't be easily replaced. You have knowledge that saves lives and solves problems. You have relationships that create opportunities. You have job security that most people would kill for. Why wouldn't that have value?"

Cara leaned back in her seat. "Here's what Don the financial advisor doesn't understand: you're not starting from zero or even starting from behind. You're starting from a position of incredible strength. You have intangible assets waiting to be realized."

Olivia sat taller.

"But I still only have very little actual money," she said.

"Right now, yes. But you have over a million dollars in assets that can be leveraged to generate money. That's completely different from having nothing."

Cara started the car. "Come on. Let's go somewhere we can really talk about this. Once you understand what you actually own, we can start talking about how to turn those assets into the financial security you want."

As they drove away from Don's office, Olivia found herself daydreaming about more money in her bank account.

She wasn't financially behind. She wasn't starting from zero. She was a professional with valuable assets who just needed to learn how to deploy them strategically.

Anxiety, shame and desperation had quietly been replaced.

She started to feel powerful.

The Hidden Assets Revolution

The financial industry's approach to net worth calculation is fundamentally flawed for professionals like nurses. Traditional advisors focus exclusively on financial assets—things you can deposit in banks or sell on markets—while completely ignoring the most valuable assets that healthcare professionals possess.

This creates a devastating psychological impact. Nurses walk away from financial consultations feeling behind, inadequate, and hopeless, when in reality they're sitting on wealth-building advantages waiting to be leveraged that most people lack entirely.

Let me show you how to calculate your true net worth as a nurse, including assets that traditional financial planning completely overlooks.

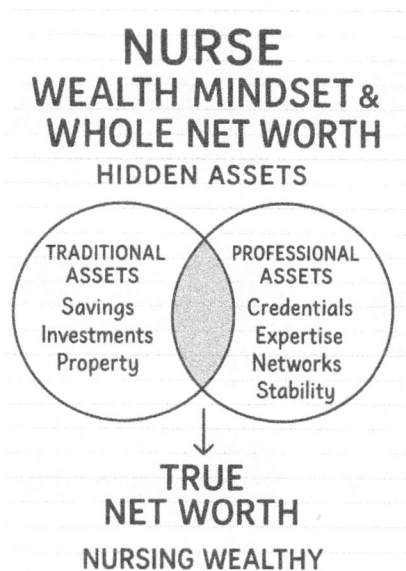

NURSE
WEALTH MINDSET &
WHOLE NET WORTH
HIDDEN ASSETS

TRADITIONAL
ASSETS
Savings
Investments
Property

PROFESSIONAL
ASSETS
Credentials
Expertise
Networks
Stability

↓
TRUE
NET WORTH
NURSING WEALTHY

Traditional Net Worth vs. True Professional Net Worth

Traditional calculation: Financial assets minus debts = Net worth

Professional calculation: Financial assets + Professional assets + Expertise value + Network value + Income stability value - Debts = True net worth

The difference is often more than $1 million, even for nurses who feel financially struggling.

Professional Asset Category 1: Licensing and Credentials

Your nursing license isn't just a piece of paper—it's a portable asset that provides access to employment opportunities unavailable to 95% of the population.

Income Mobility Value: Your license allows you to work in any province or state, most countries, and across dozens of healthcare settings. This geographic and sector flexibility has enormous economic value during recessions, personal crises, or when seeking advancement.

Recession-Proof Security: While other industries shed workers during economic downturns, healthcare demand increases. Your license represents job security that's virtually unprecedented in the modern economy.

Crisis Activation Premium: During healthcare crises, nursing expertise commands premium compensation. COVID demonstrated this dramatically—travel nurses earned $5,000-10,000 weekly when their skills were most needed.

Conservative valuation for basic nursing license: $300,000-500,000

Specialty certifications may add value:
- CCRN (Critical Care): +$150,000
- CEN (Emergency): +$150,000
- CRNA (Anesthesia): +$800,000
- Nurse Practitioner: +$600,000

Professional Asset Category 2: Specialized Expertise

Your clinical knowledge represents intellectual property that has market value far beyond your current salary.

Problem-Solving Capability: Years of nursing experience develop pattern recognition, crisis management, and decision-making skills that are valuable across industries, not just healthcare.

Training and Education Value: Your ability to teach, mentor, and transfer knowledge to others creates consulting and education opportunities.

Process Improvement Expertise: Nurses understand healthcare workflows, inefficiencies, and improvement opportunities better than most consultants who charge $200+ per hour for similar insights.

Quality and Safety Knowledge: Your understanding of patient safety, error prevention, and quality improvement has significant value to healthcare organizations, technology companies, and consulting firms.

Conservative valuation for 5+ years nursing expertise: $200,000-400,000

Professional Asset Category 3: Network Value

Your professional relationships represent hidden wealth that most nurses never recognize or leverage.

Access to Opportunities: Your network provides early access to job openings, consulting projects, and business partnerships that never reach public job boards.

Referral Income Potential: Strong professional relationships generate referrals for independent consulting, teaching, or business opportunities.

Collaboration Multiplier: Your network enables partnerships and joint ventures that multiply your individual earning potential.

Knowledge Acceleration: Professional relationships provide ongoing education and insider knowledge about industry trends, opportunities, and best practices.

Conservative valuation for established nursing network: $100,000-300,000

Professional Asset Category 4: Income Stability Premium

The predictability and security of nursing income has significant economic value that traditional financial planning undervalues.

Recession Resistance: Your ability to maintain income during economic downturns allows for more aggressive investment strategies and long-term planning.

Geographic Portability: You can relocate for personal or economic reasons without career disruption, providing flexibility that many professionals lack.

Schedule Flexibility: Shift work, per diem options, and part-time opportunities allow for income optimization and pursuit of additional opportunities.

Crisis Premium Potential: Your skills become more valuable, not less, during healthcare emergencies, providing natural hedge against economic uncertainty.

Conservative valuation: Annual salary × 10-15 (reflecting stability premium)

The Compound Effect of Professional Assets

The most powerful aspect of professional assets is how they compound and multiply each other:

- Your expertise makes your network more valuable
- Your network creates opportunities to monetize your expertise
- Your licensing provides access to higher-value positions that enhance your expertise
- Your income stability allows for investment risks that accelerate wealth building

This compound effect means your true net worth grows faster than traditional assets alone.

Why Financial Advisors Miss This

Traditional financial advisors are trained to work with assets they can directly manage and charge fees on. They can't manage your nursing license or charge commission on your professional network, so they ignore these assets entirely.

This creates a fundamental mismatch between how they evaluate your financial position and your actual wealth-building potential. They see you as financially behind when you're actually asset-rich in ways they can't measure.

Leveraging Professional Assets for Wealth Building

Understanding your true net worth isn't just a psychological boost—it's strategic information that changes how you approach wealth building.

Asset Leverage Strategy 1: Network Monetization Your professional relationships aren't just social connections—they're a market research database that reveals unmet needs and business opportunities.

Asset Leverage Strategy 2: Expertise Productization Your clinical knowledge can be packaged into educational products, consulting services, and digital resources that generate income beyond direct patient care.

Asset Leverage Strategy 3: Income Stability Optimization Your crisis-proof income allows for more aggressive investment strategies and entrepreneurial risks that would be dangerous for people with volatile incomes.

Asset Leverage Strategy 4: Geographic Arbitrage Your portable license enables strategic moves to lower-cost areas or higher-paying markets that can dramatically improve your financial position.

Reframing Your Financial Journey

When you understand your true net worth you can change how you approach wealth building:

- You're not starting from zero—you're starting with intangible assets
- You're not behind—you're asset-rich in ways traditional calculations miss
- You're not limited to your current salary—you have multiple assets to leverage
- You're not financially inadequate—you're a professional with significant unrealized wealth

This reframe is crucial because it changes your relationship with money from scarcity and desperation to abundance and opportunity. You just need to learn to leverage your assets.

The Confidence Factor

Perhaps the most valuable aspect of calculating your true net worth is the confidence it generates. When you know you possess assets worth over $1 million, you negotiate differently. You take calculated risks. You invest in yourself and your future.

You stop operating from financial fear and start operating from financial strength.

This confidence becomes a wealth-building asset itself, enabling the bold decisions and strategic investments that separate financially successful nurses from those who remain trapped by traditional employment limitations.

Wealth Work: Calculate Your True Net Worth

Time needed: 45 minutes

Impact: Transformational - This exercise typically changes how nurses see their financial position completely

Part 1: Traditional Net Worth Assessment (10 minutes)

Assets:

- Checking/savings accounts: $_____
- Retirement accounts (401k, IRA, pension): $_____
- Investment accounts: $_____
- Real estate equity: $_____
- Vehicle value: $_____
- Other assets: $_____
- **Total Traditional Assets:** $_____

Liabilities:

- Mortgage balance: $_____
- Student loans: $_____
- Credit card debt: $_____
- Car loans: $_____
- Other debts: $_____
- **Total Liabilities:** $_____

Traditional Net Worth: Assets - Liabilities = $_____

Part 2: Professional Assets Assessment (20 minutes)

Place a check mark or number beside each item that applies to you

Licensing and Credentials Value:

- Basic nursing license: _____
- Specialty certifications (list each): _____
- Advanced degrees (NP, CRNA, etc.): _____
- Other: _____

Expertise and Knowledge Value:

- Years of nursing experience: _____
- Specialized units/populations you've worked with: _____
- Leadership experience: _____
- Teaching/mentoring experience: _____
- Other: _____

Professional Network Value:

- Healthcare professional contacts: _____
- Physician relationships: _____
- Management/administrative contacts: _____
- Industry connections (vendors, consultants, etc.): _____
- Other: _____

Income Stability Value:

- Crisis-proof stability: _____

Professional Assets Total: _____

Part 3: Reflection and Integration (10 minutes)

1. **Mindset Shift:** How does seeing your professional assets change how you feel about your financial position?

2. **Asset Recognition:** Which professional assets surprised you most? Which ones had you never considered valuable before?
3. **Leverage Opportunities:** Looking at your professional assets, which ones could you most easily leverage to generate additional income?
4. **Confidence Impact:** How might knowing you can leverage your professional assets change how you:
   - Negotiate salary or contracts?
   - Consider career opportunities?
   - Approach investment decisions?
   - View your professional worth?
5. **Strategic Planning:** If you truly believed you possessed over $1 million in assets, what would you do differently in the next six months?

Part 4: Asset Leverage Planning

Choose ONE professional asset to focus on leveraging in the next 90 days:

Asset I'll focus on: _____

Specific action I'll take: _____

Potential income opportunity: $_____

Timeline for implementation: _____

Part 5: Paradigm Shift Commitment

Complete this statement: "Instead of thinking I'm financially behind, I now understand that I'm _____ and my next step is to _____."

Coming Next: In Chapter 4, Olivia discovers that her most valuable resource isn't time—it's energy. She'll learn why working harder actually makes her poorer and how to optimize her energy for maximum wealth-building impact. You'll discover the energy management strategies that separate nurses who stay trapped in the overtime cycle from those who build lasting financial freedom.

UNLOCK YOUR BONUS RESOURCES

Scan to access your exclusive webinar on building financial freedom in nursing, plus downloadable tools and templates at

www.maryghazarian.com/nursingwealthy

CHAPTER 4

E - ENERGY MANAGEMENT

"You can have all the wealth-building strategies in the world,
but without energy to execute them, they're worthless."

Olivia's Story

OLIVIA STOOD IN THE SUPPLY ROOM AT 3 AM, STARING AT A SHELF of IV tubing while trying to remember what she'd come in there to get. Her brain felt like it was wrapped in cotton, every thought requiring tremendous effort to form. This was her fifth consecutive twelve-hour shift, and somewhere around hour fifty-eight, her cognitive function had shifted from sharp to sluggish.

She'd volunteered for the extra shifts after her conversation with Cara about her true net worth. If she possessed all these valuable assets, she reasoned, working more would help her convert them into actual money faster. The overtime pay would give her breathing room to start implementing some of the wealth-building strategies they'd discussed.

But standing in the supply room, unable to remember whether she needed a 16-gauge or 18-gauge IV catheter for room 12, Olivia realized she might have made a critical miscalculation.

Her phone buzzed with a text from Mickey: *Madison asking when mommy comes home. Told her maybe tomorrow?*

Olivia felt a stab of guilt that pierced through her exhaustion. Madison had been asleep when she left for work yesterday morning. She'd be asleep when Olivia finally got home tomorrow morning. Between this stretch of shifts and the double she'd picked up last weekend, she'd seen her daughter awake for maybe two hours in the past week.

"There you are," said Rebecca, one of the newer ICU nurses, appearing in the doorway. "Room 12 needs his IV replaced, and his family is asking a million questions about the ventilator settings."

Right. IV catheter. That's what she'd come for.

Olivia grabbed an 18-gauge and headed back to room 12, where Mr. George lay intubated and sedated, his family clustered around the bedside with worried expressions. His daughter intercepted her before she reached the IV pump.

"Excuse me, the other nurse said his oxygen levels dropped earlier? Is that normal? Should we be worried? The doctor said something about PEEP settings, but we don't understand what that means..."

Usually, Olivia excelled at family education. She could explain complex medical concepts in understandable terms, provide reassurance without false hope, and help families navigate the emotional chaos of having a loved one in the ICU. It was one of her strengths as a nurse.

But standing there at hour fifty-eight, she felt her usual empathy and communication skills replaced by irritation and impatience.

"The respiratory therapist already adjusted his ventilator settings," she said curtly, focusing on the IV insertion rather than making eye contact with the family. "His oxygen levels are fine now."

She could feel the daughter's dissatisfaction with the brief explanation, but she didn't have the mental energy to do better. Every interaction felt like it was draining a battery that was already dangerously low.

The IV insertion took three attempts. Normally, Olivia could hit a vein on the first try, even in difficult patients. But her hands were shaking slightly from caffeine and fatigue, and her concentration kept wandering. By the third attempt, Mr. George's daughter was looking openly concerned about the nurse's competence.

When her shift finally ended at 7:30 AM (thirty minutes late because of a last-minute admission), Olivia sat in her car in the parking garage, too exhausted to start the engine. She pulled out her phone to check her banking app.

The overtime deposit was there: $1,847 for the five-day stretch. After taxes, probably around $1,400. It felt substantial until she calculated the cost.

Five days of barely seeing Madison. Five days of surviving on vending machine food and energy drinks. Five days of providing sub-optimal patient care since she was running on fumes. Three near-misses with medication dosing when her brain couldn't maintain focus. One family interaction that left them feeling dismissed and concerned.

And for what? $1,400 that would go toward credit card payments and Madison's school clothes, only to leave her exactly where she started financially but significantly more depleted physically and emotionally.

Olivia finally started the car and drove home, her mind cycling through a revelation: working more wasn't making her wealthier. It was making her poorer in every way that actually mattered.

When she got home, Mickey was getting Madison ready for school. Madison ran to hug her, chattering excitedly about an art project she'd made yesterday.

"Look, mommy! I drew our family!" Madison held up a picture of three stick figures standing in front of a house. "That's you, and that's daddy, and that's me!"

Olivia looked at the drawing more closely. The figure representing her was noticeably smaller than the others and colored in light pencil strokes, barely visible on the page.

"Why did you draw mommy so light?" Olivia asked.

"Because you're not here very much," Madison said matter-of-factly. "You're like a ghost mommy."

Olivia winced. She looked at Mickey, who offered a sympathetic smile but didn't contradict their daughter's assessment.

Holding back tears, Olivia gave her daughter a long hug. Then, with drawing in hand, excused herself to take a shower. She found herself sitting on the edge of the bathtub, staring at Madison's drawing, and finally understanding what Cara had been trying to tell her about energy management.

She was optimizing for the wrong variable. She'd been focused on maximizing hours worked when she should have been optimizing for energy preserved and strategically deployed.

Working five twelve-hour shifts in a row didn't make her five times more productive—it made her increasingly less effective with each passing hour. The nurse who'd fumbled three IV attempts and dismissed worried family members wasn't the same nurse who could command premium rates for consulting or teaching. That nurse—the competent, empathetic, sharp-thinking professional—only existed when she had adequate energy to deploy her skills effectively.

Olivia pulled out her phone and deleted the text she'd been about to send to her manager about picking up another shift this weekend. Instead, she opened a new note and started typing:

> *Energy Management Priorities: 1. Protect sleep and recovery time 2. Work when I'm sharp, not when I'm desperate 3. Use peak energy for wealth-building activities 4. Stop trading health and family time for overtime pay*

Olivia had jolted out of her autopilot mode that had been giving her the same results week after week. She was thinking strategically instead of just reacting to financial pressure. She was starting to understand that wealth wasn't built through exhaustion—it was built through the intelligent deployment of energy toward high-value activities.

The question was: how would she restructure her entire approach to work and money around this insight?

Why Working Harder Makes You Poorer

The overtime trap we discussed in chapter 1 is one of the most destructive patterns in nursing, disguised as a solution to financial problems when it's actually the cause of wealth stagnation. Understanding why this happens requires examining the hidden costs of trading energy for money.

The Energy Depletion Cycle

Energy is one of your most finite and valuable resources, yet most nurses treat it as unlimited. This creates a vicious cycle that destroys wealth-building capacity:

Stage 1: Financial Pressure Money concerns lead to accepting overtime shifts, extra responsibilities, or additional part-time work.

Stage 2: Energy Depletion Extended work hours drain physical, mental, and emotional energy, reducing decision-making capacity and increasing stress.

Stage 3: Poor Financial Decisions Exhaustion leads to expensive convenience purchases, impulse buying, and failure to implement wealth-building strategies.

Stage 4: Increased Financial Pressure Poor decisions create more financial stress, leading back to accepting more overtime.

Stage 5: Reduced Earning Potential Chronic exhaustion decreases professional performance, limiting advancement opportunities and premium income possibilities.

The Hidden Math of Overtime

As discussed in Chapter 1, when nurses calculate overtime value, they typically focus only on the hourly premium (time-and-a-half) while ignoring the hidden costs that often make overtime financially destructive.

True Cost Analysis:

Immediate Costs:

- Higher tax brackets reduce net pay increase
- Childcare expenses for extended hours
- Transportation costs for additional commute days
- Meal costs due to inability to meal prep when exhausted

Opportunity Costs:

- Lost time for wealth-building activities
- Reduced capacity for strategic career planning
- Inability to pursue education or certification opportunities
- Lost family time that affects relationships and mental health

Health Costs:

- Medical expenses related to stress and exhaustion
- Reduced immune function leading to more illness
- Physical wear that shortens career longevity
- Mental health impacts from chronic overwork

Performance Costs:

- Reduced quality of work affecting advancement potential
- Increased error risk that could impact professional reputation
- Decreased creativity and problem-solving capacity
- Lower energy for networking and relationship building

When all costs are calculated, overtime often generates less than $15 per hour in real value while consuming the energy needed for wealth-building activities that could generate much higher returns.

Energy vs. Time: The Critical Distinction

Most financial advice focuses on time management, but for nurses, energy management is far more critical. You can have unlimited time but accomplish nothing if you lack the energy to think clearly and act strategically.

THE NURSE'S
ENERGY INVESTMENT
PORTFOLIO

SPEND | INVEST

daily tasks | well-being
obligations | growth
distractions | purpose

**NURSING
WEALTHY**

Peak Energy Characteristics:
- Clear thinking and good judgment
- Creativity and problem-solving ability
- Confidence and communication skills
- Motivation and follow-through capacity
- Ability to learn and retain new information

Depleted Energy Characteristics:
- Poor decision-making and impulsive choices
- Reduced creativity and limited perspective
- Communication difficulties and irritability
- Procrastination and incomplete tasks
- Difficulty learning or implementing new strategies

The same person can have dramatically different wealth-building capacity depending on their energy state. Peak energy Olivia can negotiate salary increases, develop business ideas, and make strategic investments. Depleted energy Olivia orders takeout, avoids financial planning, and makes impulsive purchases.

The Peak Performance Strategy

Instead of maximizing hours worked, wealthy nurses optimize for peak performance periods and protect their energy like the precious resource it is.

Energy Audit Process:

Step 1: Track Energy Patterns For two weeks, rate your energy level every two hours on a scale of 1-10. Note:
- Time of day
- Activities leading up to that moment
- Work schedule impacts
- Sleep quality effects
- Stress level influences

Step 2: Identify Peak Windows Most nurses have 2-4 hours daily of peak energy when they're mentally sharp and emotionally resilient. These windows are your wealth-building gold mines.

Step 3: Protect Peak Energy Reserve your highest energy periods for activities that build long-term wealth:
- Financial planning and investment research
- Skill development and education
- Networking and relationship building
- Business development activities
- Strategic career planning

Step 4: Batch Low-Energy Tasks Use depleted energy periods for routine activities that don't require peak performance:
- Administrative tasks
- Household maintenance
- Passive learning (reading, listening to podcasts)
- Recovery and restoration activities

The Shift Work Advantage

While shift work creates energy management challenges, it also provides advantages that can be leveraged for wealth building when understood properly.

Block Schedule Benefits:

- Concentrated work periods followed by extended recovery time
- Ability to schedule wealth-building activities during business hours
- Flexibility to pursue education or business opportunities
- Time for strategic planning between work periods

Energy Recovery Strategies:

- Immediate post-shift recovery (first 4-6 hours)
- Active restoration (exercise, nutrition, social connection)
- Strategic rest (quality sleep in optimal environment)
- Preparation for next work period

Wealth-Building Integration:

- Schedule high-energy wealth activities during your strongest days off
- Use work breaks for micro-learning and skill development
- Leverage unusual schedules for networking with business professionals
- Plan major financial decisions during peak energy periods

The Compound Effect of Energy Optimization

When you protect and strategically deploy your energy, the effects compound rapidly:

Immediate Benefits:

- Better performance at work, leading to advancement opportunities
- Improved decision-making reducing costly mistakes
- Increased capacity for wealth-building activities
- Better relationships due to emotional availability

Medium-term Benefits:
- Faster skill development and career progression
- Successful implementation of wealth-building strategies
- Improved health reducing medical expenses
- Stronger professional network creating opportunities

Long-term Benefits:
- Sustainable career that doesn't burn out
- Multiple income streams developed during peak energy periods
- Strong family relationships that provide support and motivation
- Financial security that reduces stress and preserves energy

Breaking the Overtime Addiction

Many nurses become psychologically dependent on overtime, using it as their primary financial strategy. Breaking this addiction requires both practical and psychological changes.

Practical Steps:
1. Calculate the true cost of overtime including all hidden expenses
2. Identify fixed expenses that can be reduced to decrease overtime dependency
3. Develop alternative income sources that don't require trading time for money
4. Create systems that automate wealth-building during peak energy periods

Psychological Shifts:
1. Recognize that working more isn't the same as earning more
2. Understand that rest and recovery are investments, not laziness
3. Accept that saying no to overtime enables yes to better opportunities
4. Believe that your expertise has value beyond hourly wages

The Energy Investment Portfolio

Like financial investing, energy management requires diversification across different types of restoration and optimization activities.

Physical Energy (40%):

- Quality sleep in optimal environment
- Regular exercise that energizes rather than depletes
- Nutrition that supports sustained energy
- Healthcare that prevents rather than treats problems

Mental Energy (30%):

- Stress management practices that prevent accumulation
- Learning activities that stimulate rather than overwhelm
- Creative outlets that restore cognitive function
- Strategic thinking time for planning and reflection

Emotional Energy (20%):

- Relationships that support rather than drain
- Activities that provide joy and fulfillment
- Boundaries that protect from energy vampires
- Practices that build resilience and emotional intelligence

Spiritual/Purpose Energy (10%):

- Activities that connect to larger meaning and purpose
- Service that fulfills rather than depletes
- Growth experiences that expand perspective
- Reflection practices that maintain perspective and motivation

When these categories are balanced, you create sustainable energy that supports both excellent patient care and wealth-building activities.

Wealth Work: Your Energy Optimization Plan

Time needed: 60 minutes

Impact: Foundational - Energy optimization enables all other wealth-building strategies

Part 1: Energy Audit (20 minutes)

For the next 7 days, track your energy using this simple scale every 2 hours while awake:

Energy Scale:

- **4 (Peak):** Mentally sharp, creative, confident, motivated
- **3 (Good):** Alert, focused, capable of complex tasks
- **2 (Low):** Functional but not optimal, easily distracted
- **1 (Depleted):** Exhausted, poor judgment, operating on autopilot

Daily Tracking Sheet:

Day 1: ___/___/___

6 AM: Energy   ___ | Activity: _____

8 AM: Energy   ___ | Activity: _____

10 AM: Energy   ___ | Activity: _____

12 PM: Energy   ___ | Activity: _____

2 PM: Energy   ___ | Activity: _____

4 PM: Energy   ___ | Activity: _____

6 PM: Energy   ___ | Activity: _____

8 PM: Energy   ___ | Activity: _____

10 PM: Energy   ___ | Activity: _____

Sleep Quality: ___/10

Work Schedule: Day/Night/Off

Stress Level: ___/10

Part 2: Pattern Recognition (15 minutes)

After 7 days of tracking, analyze your patterns:

Peak Energy Times:

- When do you consistently rate 4/4 or 3/4? _____
- How many peak hours do you have per day? _____
- What activities or conditions support peak energy? _____

Energy Drains:

- When do you consistently rate 1/4 or 2/4? _____
- What activities or conditions deplete your energy fastest?

- How does your work schedule affect your energy patterns?

Recovery Patterns:

- How long does it take to recover from work shifts?

- What activities help restore your energy most effectively?

- When do you feel most energized on your days off?

Part 3: Energy Investment Analysis (10 minutes)

Current Energy Allocation: What percentage of your peak energy hours are currently spent on:

- Direct patient care: _____%
- Administrative/routine work tasks: _____%
- Household/family responsibilities: _____%
- Wealth-building activities: _____%
- Rest/recovery/personal care: _____%

Other: _____%

Wealth-Building Opportunity:

- How many peak energy hours per week could you realistically redirect to wealth-building? _____
- What low-energy activities are you currently doing during peak times? _____

Part 4: Energy Protection Plan (15 minutes)

Peak Energy Commitments: For the next 30 days, I commit to using my peak energy hours for:

1. _____
2. _____
3. _____

Energy Drains to Eliminate: I will stop or reduce these energy-depleting activities:

1. _____
2. _____
3. _____

Recovery Investments: I will invest in these energy-restoring activities:

1. _____
2. _____
3. _____

Boundary Setting: I will protect my energy by:

- Saying no to: _____
- Limiting: _____
- Scheduling: _____

Part 5: The Overtime Analysis

True Overtime Cost Calculation:

Last month's overtime:

- Extra hours worked: _____
- Gross overtime pay: $_____
- Additional taxes (estimate 30-35%): $_____
- Childcare/transportation costs: $_____
- Convenience food/purchases due to exhaustion: $_____
- **Net overtime value:** $_____

Opportunity Cost Assessment:

- How many peak energy hours were consumed by overtime?

  _____

- What wealth-building activities were postponed or cancelled?

  _____

- How did the extra work affect your family relationships?

  _____

- How did exhaustion impact your performance in your regular job?

  _____

Alternative Strategy: If you used those same peak energy hours for wealth-building instead of overtime, what could you potentially accomplish?

Part 6: 30-Day Energy Experiment

Choose ONE change to implement for the next 30 days:

Option A: Peak Energy Protection Commit to using your top 2 peak energy hours daily for wealth-building activities instead of routine tasks.

Option B: Overtime Reduction Reduce overtime by 25% and invest that time in energy restoration and wealth-building preparation.

Option C: Recovery Optimization Implement a systematic recovery routine after each work shift to restore energy faster and more completely.

My 30-day experiment: _____

Success measurement: _____

Weekly check-in schedule: _____

Coming Next: In Chapter 5, Olivia learns to make her money work as hard as she does through strategic asset building designed specifically for healthcare professionals. She'll discover investment approaches that account for shift work schedules, risk tolerance shaped by medical training, and the unique advantages that nurses possess in building long-term wealth.

A

CHAPTER 5

A - ASSET BUILDING & STRATEGIC INVESTMENTS

"Asset building is about creating systems that build
wealth whether you're working or sleeping."

Olivia's Story

OLIVIA SAT IN HER CAR OUTSIDE A BIG BOX STORE, STARING AT HER phone with a mixture of excitement and terror. She'd just downloaded an investment app that Cara had recommended, and now she was looking at a screen asking her to "Choose your risk tolerance" and "Select your investment timeline."

Three months had passed since she'd started optimizing her energy instead of maximizing her overtime hours. She was working her regular three twelve-hour shifts per week, protecting her peak energy times for family and financial planning, and—most surprisingly—actually had money left over at the end of each month for the first time in years.

Not a lot of money. But $400 that wasn't immediately consumed by bills or unexpected expenses felt like a fortune compared to the financial stress she'd lived with for so long.

The investment app was asking her to choose between "Conservative," "Moderate," and "Aggressive" investment strategies. Olivia had no idea what any of those meant in practical terms. She'd googled "how to invest money for beginners" and been overwhelmed by articles about index funds, expense ratios, and asset allocation that might as well have been written in a foreign language.

Her phone rang. Cara.

"Hey! How's the investment research going?"

"I'm sitting in a parking lot and my mind is going in circles about risk tolerance," Olivia admitted. "This app wants me to make all these decisions about things I don't understand. What if I pick wrong and lose all our money?"

Cara laughed. "Remember when you were a new grad and everything about nursing felt overwhelming? Did you quit because you didn't know everything on your first day?"

"No, but this is different. If I make a mistake with a patient, I can call for help or fix it immediately. If I make a mistake with our money..."

"Olivia, you make life-and-death decisions every shift. You manage multiple critical patients simultaneously. You can learn to pick some basic investments."

Cara was right, but it didn't make the decision feel less intimidating. "Can you just tell me what to choose?"

"I could, but that wouldn't help you understand why. Besides, your situation is different from mine. Let me ask you this: what do you know about risk as a nurse that might apply to investing?"

Olivia thought about it. "We assess risk constantly. We balance the risks of treatment against the risks of not treating. We monitor for complications and adjust when things change."

"Exactly. So let's apply that thinking to your investments. What's the risk of not investing at all?"

"I guess... inflation? My money loses purchasing power over time?"

"Right. And what's your timeline for needing this money?"

"Not for decades. This is supposed to be for retirement."

"So you have time to recover from short-term fluctuations. What else do you know about your situation that might affect your risk tolerance?"

Olivia considered this. "I have job security. Nursing isn't going any-where. Even if the economy crashes, people still get sick."

"That's huge, Olivia. Your income stability means you can take more investment risk than someone whose job might disappear in a recession. You don't need to keep everything in 'safe' investments that barely keep up with inflation."

Cara continued, "Here's what I want you to do. Don't think about this as 'Conservative versus Aggressive.' Think about it as 'What mix of investments matches my nursing advantages?'"

Olivia began to understand her situation. Instead of seeing investing as a foreign concept she had to master, she started viewing it as another type of assessment and care planning—skills she already possessed.

"What do you mean about nursing advantages?"

"You understand healthcare from the inside. You know which technologies actually improve patient care versus which ones are just marketing hype. You've seen how healthcare companies operate. You understand healthcare trends before they hit the mainstream financial news."

Olivia had never thought about her clinical knowledge as investment knowledge. "So I should invest in healthcare companies?"

"Maybe some. But more importantly, you should leverage what you know about healthcare to make informed investment decisions across all sectors. Plus, your stable income means you can invest consistently even when markets are volatile. It's called dollar-cost averaging"

Cara guided her through the app's questions, helping her translate nursing thinking into investment decisions. Moderate risk tolerance made sense—she was comfortable with calculated risks when she under-stood the reasoning. A long-term timeline fit her career stage. Automatic monthly investments aligned with her energy management goals.

Within twenty minutes, Olivia had set up automatic transfers of $400 monthly into a diversified portfolio of low-cost index funds, with a small allocation to healthcare sector investments that she could understand and monitor using her professional knowledge.

Olivia felt proud. She'd finally started investing, and she'd realized that nursing had already taught her the foundational concepts she needed to build wealth. Risk assessment, systematic monitoring, long-term planning, adapting strategies based on changing conditions—these were skills she used every day at work.

Over the next few weeks, Olivia found herself checking her investment account with the same attention she paid to her patients' vital signs. Some days the balance was up, some days it was down. She was learning to see these fluctuations as normal variations rather than emergencies requiring immediate intervention. Cara assured her to not make sudden changes in the plan based on emotion as ups and downs in the market on a daily basis are expected. So long as the overall trend was growth.

Six months later, Olivia was sitting in the same coffee shop where Cara had first challenged her thinking about money, but now the conversation had a completely different tone.

"I can't believe I waited so long to start investing," Olivia said, showing Cara her account balance on her phone. "It's only been six months, but seeing the money grow—even a little—feels like magic."

"How much have you invested total?"

"$2,400. But the account shows $2,547. That's $147 I didn't have to work for."

Cara smiled. "That $147 represents your money working while you sleep. Imagine that growing over the next twenty years."

Olivia was already doing the math. "If I keep investing $400 monthly and get average returns... Cara, I could have over $300,000 by the time I retire."

"Now you're thinking like a wealthy nurse. But here's the really exciting part—$400 a month is just your starting point. As your income grows and you develop additional income streams, you can invest more.

The nurses who build serious wealth aren't just putting away a few hundred dollars a month forever."

Olivia leaned forward. "What do you mean?"

"Remember when we calculated your true net worth? All those professional assets you possess? It's time to start converting some of those into additional income that you can invest."

Cara pulled out her notebook again. "The nurses I know who've built real wealth—six figures and beyond—they all have the same pattern. They start exactly where you are now, with systematic investing of whatever they can afford. But then they leverage their nursing expertise to create additional income streams that accelerate their wealth building."

"Like what?"

"Teaching continuing education courses. Consulting on healthcare projects. Creating online resources for other nurses. Freelance writing for medical publications. The opportunities are endless when you start thinking of your expertise as a business asset."

Olivia smiled at the thought of building something of her own. "I hadn't thought about that. I've just been focused on investing what I can save from my regular salary."

"Which is a great foundation. But imagine if you could invest $800 a month instead of $400. Or $1,200. What would that do to your twenty-year projection?"

Olivia did the mental calculation. "That would be... over half a million dollars."

"Now you're starting to understand why some nurses retire as millionaires while others struggle financially their entire careers. It's not about their base salary—it's about their understanding of how to leverage nursing expertise into wealth-building opportunities."

As they left the coffee shop that day, Olivia realized she'd crossed another psychological threshold. Six months ago, investing had felt impossible and intimidating. Now it felt natural and exciting. But more importantly, she was starting to see investment as just the first step in a much larger wealth-building strategy.

She wasn't just a nurse who happened to invest some money. She was becoming a nurse who understood how to systematically build wealth using every advantage her profession provided.

The next question was: what would she do with this newfound confidence?

The Nursing Advantage in Asset Building

Traditional financial advice treats all investors the same, ignoring the unique advantages that healthcare professionals possess. This generic approach causes nurses to miss opportunities perfectly suited to their profession, risk tolerance, and knowledge base.

Understanding and leveraging your nursing advantages transforms investing from intimidating guesswork into strategic wealth building based on skills you already possess.

Advantage 1: Crisis-Proof Income Foundation

Your nursing income provides stability that most investors lack, creating opportunities for wealth-building strategies that would be dangerous for people with volatile incomes.

Consistent Investment Capacity: Unlike professionals whose income fluctuates with economic cycles, you can invest systematically through market downturns. This enables dollar-cost averaging—buying more shares when prices are low and fewer when prices are high, which improves long-term returns.

Emergency Fund Efficiency: Traditional advice recommends 6-12 months of expenses in emergency funds. Your job security allows for smaller emergency reserves (3-6 months), freeing more money for growth investments.

Risk Tolerance Optimization: Your stable income allows for more aggressive investment strategies early in your career. While other professionals must prioritize safety due to income uncertainty, you can pursue growth investments with confidence that your nursing income will continue regardless of market conditions.

Market Timing Immunity: You can ignore short-term market volatility if your investment timeline is measured in decades, not months. Your ability to continue investing through recessions gives you significant advantages over emotional investors who stop contributing during market downturns.

Advantage 2: Healthcare Industry Expertise

Your clinical knowledge provides investment insights that financial advisors often lack, enabling informed decisions about one of the economy's largest and most stable sectors.

Healthcare Sector Intelligence: You understand which medical technologies actually improve patient outcomes versus marketing hype. You see emerging healthcare trends in real-time through your daily practice. You understand healthcare economics from the inside, including which cost-cutting measures are sustainable and which compromise quality.

Technology Assessment: You can evaluate healthcare technology investments based on practical utility rather than promotional materials. You understand regulatory requirements and adoption challenges that affect healthcare company success. You recognize innovations that solve real clinical problems versus those that sound impressive but lack practical application.

Demographic Trend Recognition: Your patient care experience reveals demographic shifts and healthcare needs before they become investment themes. You understand aging population impacts on healthcare demand. You see chronic disease trends that drive long-term healthcare growth.

Company Quality Assessment: Your experience with different healthcare vendors helps you evaluate company management, customer service, and product quality—factors that affect long-term investment performance.

Advantage 3: Risk Assessment and Management Skills

Your clinical training provides sophisticated risk analysis capabilities that transfer directly to investment decisions.

Risk-Benefit Analysis: You routinely weigh treatment risks against potential benefits, skills that apply directly to investment evaluation. You understand that avoiding all risk often creates different but equally serious risks. You can assess multiple variables simultaneously to make optimal decisions under uncertainty.

Systematic Monitoring: Your patient monitoring skills translate to portfolio monitoring—watching for concerning trends while avoiding overreaction to normal fluctuations. You understand the difference between expected variations and true emergencies requiring intervention.

Evidence-Based Decision Making: Your training in evidence-based practice helps you distinguish between investment marketing and actual performance data. You can critically evaluate financial research using the same analytical skills you apply to medical research.

Long-Term Outcome Focus: Your understanding of treatment progressions helps you maintain long-term investment perspectives despite short-term volatility.

Strategic Investment Approaches for Nurses

These approaches leverage your nursing advantages while addressing the unique challenges of healthcare careers.

Foundation Strategy: Automated Wealth Building

Emergency Fund Sizing:

- 3-4 months expenses (versus 6-12 months for less stable careers)
- High-yield savings account earning 4-5% annually
- Accessible but separate from everyday banking

Retirement Account Optimization:

- Maximize employer retirement savings account matching immediately
- Consider tax-free growth accounts
- Automate contributions to eliminate decision fatigue

Systematic Investment Plan:

- Start with any amount ($25-50 monthly if necessary)
- Increase contributions by $25-50 every three months
- Target 15-20% total savings rate (including retirement matching)
- Use automatic transfers to eliminate emotional decision-making

Growth Strategy: Healthcare Sector Integration

Healthcare-Focused Portfolio Allocation:

- 20-30% healthcare sector investments (leveraging your expertise)
- 60-70% broad market diversification (total stock market index funds)
- 5-10% international diversification
- 0-10% bonds (minimal for younger nurses with stable income)

Healthcare Investment Categories and examples:

Defensive Healthcare (Lower Risk):
- Large pharmaceutical companies with diverse drug portfolios
- Medical device manufacturers with established products
- Healthcare insurance companies with stable customer bases
- Hospital systems in growing markets

Growth Healthcare (Higher Risk/Reward):

- Biotech companies developing promising therapies
- Healthcare technology companies improving care delivery
- Specialized medical device companies with innovative products
- Telemedicine and digital health platforms

Healthcare ETFs (Diversified Exposure):

- Health Care Select Sector SPDR Fund (XLV)
- Vanguard Health Care ETF (VHT)
- iShares U.S. Healthcare ETF (IYH)

Acceleration Strategy: Income Diversification

Phase 1: Foundation Building (Months 1-12)

- Establish automated investment systems
- Build emergency fund to target level
- Begin healthcare sector research and education
- Start small side income experiments ($200-500 monthly)

Phase 2: Income Scaling (Months 12-36)

- Increase side income to $500-1,500 monthly
- Invest 50-75% of additional income
- Expand healthcare investment knowledge
- Consider real estate or other asset classes

Phase 3: Wealth Acceleration (Years 3+)

- Scale side income beyond $1,500 monthly
- Explore advanced investment strategies
- Consider business ownership or partnership opportunities
- Plan for financial independence timeline

Risk Management for Nurse Investors

Professional Liability Protection:

- Maintain adequate malpractice insurance
- Consider umbrella insurance policy for asset protection
- Separate business assets from personal investments
- Understand how professional licenses affect liability

Career Longevity Planning:

- Invest in continuing education and certifications
- Maintain physical health to extend career capacity
- Develop multiple income streams to reduce employment dependence
- Plan for potential career transitions or early retirement

Market Risk Mitigation:

- Diversify across asset classes and geographic regions
- Maintain investment discipline during market volatility
- Avoid emotional investment decisions based on short-term events
- Use your stable income to take advantage of market downturns

Common Investment Mistakes Nurses Make

Mistake 1: Waiting for Perfect Knowledge Nurses often delay investing because they want to understand everything before starting. The cost of waiting exceeds the risk of starting with simple, low cost, diversified investments while learning.

Mistake 2: Over-Conservative Allocation Many nurses invest too conservatively due to general risk aversion, missing growth opportunities that their stable income makes safe to pursue.

Mistake 3: Emotional Market Timing Healthcare workers may try to time investments around economic uncertainty, missing long-term growth by riding out volatile periods.

Mistake 4: Neglecting Tax Advantages Failing to maximize tax-advantaged accounts before investing in taxable accounts reduces long-term wealth accumulation significantly.

Mistake 5: Analysis Paralysis Over-researching investment options while failing to take action. Perfect investment selection matters less than consistent contribution and long-term discipline.

Mistake 6: Novice to Expert Aversion After the sometimes traumatic experience of being a novice nurse, it is hard to be a novice again. It is important to speak with experts like financial advisors, lawyers and business coaches to help you grow your financial competence and business acumen.

The Compound Effect for Nurses

Your nursing advantages create compound benefits when applied consistently over time:

Years 1-5: Foundation Building

- Automated systems eliminate decision fatigue
- Healthcare knowledge improves investment selection
- Stable income enables consistent contributions through market cycles
- Early start captures maximum compound growth

Years 5-15: Acceleration Phase

- Additional income streams significantly increase investment capacity
- Healthcare expertise enables informed sector overweighting
- Professional network creates investment opportunities
- Compound growth becomes substantial

Years 15-30: Wealth Maturation

- Multiple income streams reduce employment dependence
- Investment portfolio provides significant passive income

- Healthcare expertise creates consulting and advisory opportunities
- Financial independence becomes achievable reality

The key insight is that your nursing background provides advantages in every phase of wealth building, from initial risk assessment through long-term portfolio management. These advantages compound over time, creating wealth-building capacity that exceeds what generic financial advice suggests is possible for healthcare workers.

Wealth Work: Build Your Investment Foundation

Time needed: 90 minutes

Impact: High - This creates the automated systems that build wealth while you focus on patient care

Part 1: Foundation Assessment (20 minutes)

Current Financial Position:

Monthly take-home income:	$_____
Monthly essential expenses:	$_____
Current emergency fund:	$_____
Current retirement account balance:	$_____
Current debt payments:	$_____
Available for investing monthly:	$_____

Emergency Fund Target:

Monthly essential expenses × 4 =	$_____
Current emergency fund:	$_____
Emergency fund gap:	$_____

Investment Readiness: ☐ Emergency fund ☐ High-interest debt under control ☐ Stable monthly income ☐ Basic understanding of investment risk

Part 2: Account Setup Plan (25 minutes)

Retirement Accounts (Priority #1):

Employer Retirement Account:

- Current contribution: _____%
- Employer match available: _____%
- **Action needed:** Increase to capture full match

Tax Free Savings Account and/or Registered Retirement Savings Account:

- Year contribution limit: _____
- Monthly amount: _____
- **Action needed:** Open account and automate

Investment Account Setup: ☐ Research low-cost brokerage ☐ Open Tax Free Savings and Retirment accounts ☐ Set up automatic monthly transfer ☐ Choose initial investments (target-date fund for simplicity)

Part 3: Healthcare Investment Analysis (25 minutes)

Healthcare Knowledge Inventory: List healthcare companies/sectors you understand from your nursing experience:

Pharmaceutical/Biotech:

- Companies whose drugs you administer: _____
- Treatment areas you work with: _____
- Emerging therapies you've observed: _____

Medical Devices:

- Equipment manufacturers you use: _____
- Technology trends you've witnessed: _____
- Devices that improve patient outcomes: _____

Healthcare Services:

- Hospital systems you've worked for/with: _____
- Insurance companies you interact with: _____
- Technology platforms you use: _____

Investment Research Questions: For healthcare investments you're considering:

1. Does this solve a real clinical problem you've observed?
2. Is adoption increasing based on your professional experience?
3. Does this company have a sustainable competitive advantage?
4. Are regulatory/reimbursement trends favorable?

Part 4: Portfolio Design (20 minutes)

Basic Portfolio Allocation for Nurses:

Conservative Approach (Lower risk tolerance):

- 60% Total Stock Market Index Fund
- 20% Healthcare Sector Fund
- 15% International Stock Index Fund
- 5% Bond Index Fund

Moderate Approach (Balanced risk tolerance):

- 70% Total Stock Market Index Fund
- 20% Healthcare Sector Fund
- 10% International Stock Index Fund
- 0% Bonds (young investors with stable income)

Growth Approach (Higher risk tolerance):

- 60% Total Stock Market Index Fund
- 25% Healthcare Sector Fund
- 10% International Stock Index Fund
- 5% Individual Healthcare Stocks (companies you understand)

Your Target Allocation:

- Total Stock Market: _____%
- Healthcare Sector: _____%
- International Stocks: _____%
- Bonds: _____%
- Individual Stocks: _____%

Part 5: Automation Setup

Monthly Investment Plan:

- Emergency fund contribution: $_____
- Retirement account contribution: $_____
- Additional investment contribution: $_____
- **Total monthly wealth building:** $_____

Automation Schedule: ☐ Set up automatic transfer 2 days after payday ☐ Automate retirement account contributions ☐ Schedule quarterly portfolio review ☐ Set annual contribution increase (every January)

Part 6: Nursing-Specific Strategies

Shift Work Optimization:

- Schedule investment research during off-days when mentally fresh
- Use slow periods at work for financial education (podcasts, articles)
- Batch investment decisions quarterly to avoid decision fatigue

Healthcare Expertise Leverage:

- Subscribe to healthcare investment newsletters
- Monitor trends in your specialty area for investment insights
- Network with nurses in different specialties for broader perspective

Income Stability Advantages: ☐ Discuss with an expert whether to set up aggressive investment plan knowing income is stable ☐ Plan to invest tax refunds and overtime pay ☐ Ignore short-term market volatility

Part 7: 90-Day Action Plan

Week 1: ☐ Open investment accounts ☐ Set up automatic transfers ☐ Make first investment (even if small)

Week 2-4: ☐ Research and select specific investments ☐ Optimize employer retirement plan contributions ☐ Create system for monitoring progress

Month 2: ☐ Increase investment amount by $25-50 ☐ Begin healthcare sector research ☐ Track spending to find additional investment money

Month 3: ☐ Review and rebalance portfolio if needed ☐ Plan for quarterly contribution increase ☐ Assess progress toward emergency fund goal

First Quarterly Review Questions:

1. How do I feel about investing now versus 90 days ago?
2. What have I learned about my risk tolerance?
3. What healthcare investment opportunities have I identified?
4. How can I increase my monthly contributions?
5. What additional income streams could accelerate my wealth building?

Coming Next: In Chapter 6, Olivia discovers how to transform her nursing expertise into scalable income streams that work whether she's clocked in or sleeping. She'll learn the difference between trading time for money and creating assets that generate wealth around the clock, setting the foundation for true financial independence.

L

L - LEVERAGE & SCALE YOUR EXPERTISE

"Your nursing expertise is intellectual property waiting to be monetized. The question isn't whether you should profit from it, but how you can use it to help more nurses and patients while building wealth."

Olivia's Story

OLIVIA WAS HALFWAY THROUGH HER SECOND CUP OF COFFEE, SITting at her kitchen table on a rare Tuesday morning off, when her phone buzzed with a text from her former colleague Rajpreet.

> *"Hey! Remember that ECMO training you did for our unit last year? My new hospital needs someone to train their ICU staff on ECMO protocols. They're willing to pay $75/hour for 8 hours of training. Interested?"*

Olivia stared at the message, calculator wheels spinning in her head. $75 an hour. That was more than double her regular hourly rate, and this would be for sharing knowledge she already possessed—knowledge she'd developed through years of ICU experience and additional training she'd pursued on her own time.

But her immediate reaction surprised her: guilt.

Was it ethical to charge money for teaching other nurses? Wasn't sharing knowledge part of being a good colleague? The training she'd provided at her own hospital had been unpaid, considered part of her professional development responsibilities.

She was still mulling this over when Cara called for their weekly check-in.

"I got offered a consulting gig," Olivia said without preamble. "Teaching ECMO protocols. Seventy-five dollars an hour."

"That's fantastic! When do you start?"

"I haven't said yes yet. It feels... weird to charge for nursing knowledge."

Cara was quiet for a moment. "Olivia, when you went to that conference on advanced cardiac life support last year, how much did you pay?"

"Eight hundred dollars for two days."

"And who was teaching it?"

"Nurses and doctors with ACLS expertise."

"Did you think they were being unethical by charging for their knowledge?"

"No, that was different. That was formal education."

"How is it different? You have specialized knowledge that other nurses need. You've invested time and money developing that expertise. The hospital needs training that will improve patient care. Why shouldn't you be compensated for providing value?"

Olivia realized she was applying a double standard. When others monetized their nursing expertise, it was professional education. When she considered doing it, it felt like commercializing her caring nature.

"I guess I've never thought of my knowledge as... sellable," she admitted.

"That's exactly the mindset that keeps nurses financially limited," Cara said. "We've been conditioned to give away our expertise for free and then wonder why we're undervalued. Your ECMO knowledge doesn't just exist in a vacuum—you developed it through education, training, and experience. That has real value."

Cara continued, "Here's a question: If you don't do this training, what happens?"

"They'll probably find someone else, or use a training company."

"And if they use a training company, how much do you think that company charges?"

Olivia had no idea. "More than seventy-five an hour?"

"Try three to five hundred dollars per hour, plus travel expenses. You're not overcharging—you're probably undercharging."

That evening, Olivia researched medical education companies online. Cara was right. Corporate training programs charged hospitals $2,000-5,000 per day for the same type of specialized nursing education she'd been asked to provide.

She texted Rajpreet back: *"Yes, I'm interested. Can we discuss the details?"*

Two weeks later, Olivia found herself standing in front of twenty ICU nurses at Queensview Medical Center, leading them through ECMO setup, troubleshooting, and patient management protocols. The content came naturally—she'd lived this knowledge for years. But presenting it formally, being recognized as the expert, receiving enthusiastic questions and grateful feedback... that felt entirely new.

During the lunch break, several nurses approached her.

"Do you do training on other topics?" asked Jennifer, a charge nurse. "We could really use someone to teach mechanical ventilation basics to our newer nurses."

"Our hospital system has three other facilities that could use this ECMO training," mentioned David, an educator. "Would you be interested in developing this into a regular program?"

By the end of the day, Olivia had not only earned $600 for eight hours of training, but she'd identified potential opportunities for ongoing consulting work. And, she'd experienced something she'd never felt before: being valued as an expert rather than just a worker.

Driving home, she called Cara to debrief.

"How did it feel?" Cara asked.

"Honestly? Amazing. I felt... professional in a different way. Like my knowledge had real worth beyond just doing my job."

"That's because it does. What you experienced today is what happens when you start positioning yourself as an expert rather than just an employee."

"The weird thing is, I was helping other nurses improve their practice, which felt completely aligned with my values. It wasn't like I was abandoning caring for money—I was getting paid to help more nurses provide better patient care."

Cara laughed. "Now you're getting it. This is how you scale your impact. Instead of being an excellent nurse caring for a few patients per shift, you become an expert nurse improving the skills of dozens of other nurses who then provide better care for hundreds of patients."

"But this was just one training. It's not like I can quit my job and become a full-time educator."

"Maybe not right away. But what if you did one training per month? That's an extra $600 monthly, or $7,200 annually. What if you developed online content that could be purchased by nurses nationwide? What if you created a certification program that hospitals could license? What if you trained other nurses to deliver your content?"

Olivia's head spun. "I never thought about... building something bigger."

"Here's what I've learned: most nurses stop at the first level—trading time for money at a higher rate. But the nurses who build real wealth figure out how to scale their expertise so it generates income even when they're not actively working."

"What do you mean?"

"Online courses that sell while you sleep. Certification programs that generate ongoing licensing fees. Consulting contracts that pay for results rather than hours. Digital resources that can be sold to thousands of nurses without requiring your time for each sale."

Olivia pulled into her driveway but stayed in the car, mind racing with possibilities she'd never considered. "That sounds... big. And complicated."

"It doesn't have to start big. It starts exactly where you are today—with recognizing that your expertise has value and taking the first step to monetize it. Everything else builds from there. You don't have to know *how* to do everything. Start thinking about *who* can help you. Who in your network knows about business, education and licensing."

Who not how. Olivia thought. Olivia reached out to a former manager with an MBA for mentorship. The manager declined, stating her calendar was full, but directed her to a colleague who she felt would be a good fit.

Over the next few months, Olivia found herself saying yes to opportunities she would have automatically declined before. A second ECMO training at another hospital. A request to develop written protocols for a specialty unit. An invitation to speak at a regional nursing conference. Her new mentor supported her every step of the way.

Each opportunity built on the previous one. The written protocols led to requests for policy development. The conference presentation led to invitations from other conferences. The training work led to hospitals asking her to develop comprehensive education programs.

Six months after her first consulting gig, Olivia was earning an additional $2,000-3,000 monthly from expertise-based income. She was building a reputation as a specialist in critical care education, creating a professional identity that extended far beyond her staff nurse role.

Olivia had stopped thinking of herself as "just a staff nurse" and started thinking of herself as a critical care expert with valuable knowledge to share. This shift changed everything about how she approached her career, her finances, and her future possibilities.

She was no longer trading time for money. She was converting her expertise into scalable assets that could generate income regardless of how many shifts she worked.

And she was just getting started.

From Expert to Income Generator

The transformation Olivia experienced represents the most significant opportunity most nurses never recognize: converting professional expertise into scalable income streams. This isn't about abandoning patient care or becoming "commercial"—it's about recognizing that your nursing knowledge has market value far beyond your current employment.

The Expertise Monetization Spectrum

Nursing expertise can be monetized across a spectrum from simple time-for-money trades to completely passive income generation.

THE EXPERTISE MONETIZATION SPECTRUM

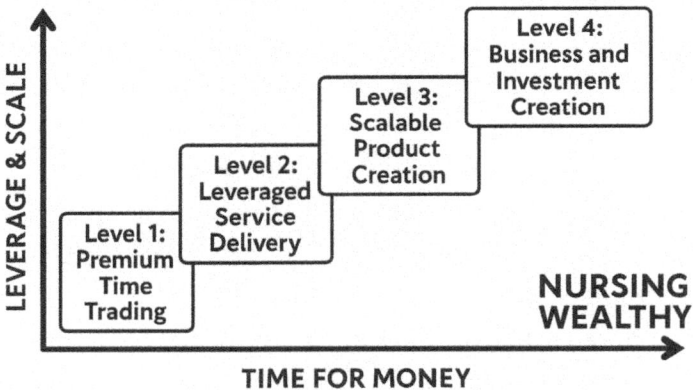

LEVERAGE & SCALE (vertical axis)

Level 1: Premium Time Trading
Level 2: Leveraged Service Delivery
Level 3: Scalable Product Creation
Level 4: Business and Investment Creation

NURSING WEALTHY

TIME FOR MONEY (horizontal axis)

Level 1: Premium Time Trading

- Consulting at higher hourly rates than regular employment
- Specialized training delivery
- Expert witness work
- Per diem work in specialized units

Level 2: Leveraged Service Delivery

- Group training programs serving multiple participants
- Online courses reaching geographically dispersed audiences

- Certification programs with ongoing renewal requirements
- Systematic consultation methodologies

Level 3: Scalable Product Creation

- Digital courses that sell without ongoing time investment
- Licensed protocols and procedures
- Subscription-based educational content
- Software or apps incorporating your expertise

Level 4: Business and Investment Creation

- Educational companies built around your methodology
- Licensing your expertise to institutions
- Investment in healthcare companies where your expertise adds value
- Partnership opportunities leveraging your professional network

The Hidden Value in Your Daily Practice

Every problem you solve routinely at work represents a potential income-generating opportunity. The key is recognizing that challenges you handle easily are struggles that keep other nurses awake at night.

Assessment and Problem-Solving Value: You've developed pattern recognition and systematic approaches to complex clinical situations. This methodology can be taught to other nurses, packaged into protocols, or consulted on by healthcare organizations.

Process Improvement Expertise: Your understanding of workflow inefficiencies, communication breakdowns, and system problems has significant value to healthcare administrators, technology companies, and quality improvement consultants.

Education and Mentorship Capabilities: Your ability to explain complex concepts, break down procedures, and help others develop competence represents intellectual property that can be systematized and scaled.

Specialized Knowledge Applications: Your expertise in specific patient populations, procedures, or technologies has market value across multiple contexts—direct education, content creation, product development, and strategic consultation.

The Mindset Shift: From Employee to Expert

The most challenging aspect of monetizing nursing expertise is psychological: shifting from employee mindset to expert positioning.

Employee Mindset:

- "I'm paid to do my job"
- "Sharing knowledge is part of being a good colleague"
- "I'm just doing what any nurse would do"
- "Charging for expertise feels wrong"

Expert Mindset:

- "My expertise has developed through significant investment and experience"
- "Sharing knowledge professionally enables me to help more people"
- "I solve problems that others struggle with"
- "Appropriate compensation enables sustainable knowledge sharing"

This shift is crucial because it affects every decision about pricing, positioning, and professional development. Experts command premium rates because they provide value that's difficult to replace.

Building Your Expertise Portfolio

Think of expertise development like building an investment portfolio—you want diverse assets that compound over time and create multiple income opportunities.

Core Competency Development: Identify 1-3 areas where you have genuine expertise that others value. This might be:

- Specific patient populations (pediatric, geriatric, critical care)
- Specialized procedures or technologies
- Quality improvement methodologies
- Leadership and management approaches
- Education and training techniques

Adjacent Skill Building: Develop complementary skills that enhance your core expertise:

- Presentation and public speaking abilities
- Writing and content creation skills
- Technology and digital platform knowledge
- Business and marketing understanding
- Project management and consultation methods

Credibility Establishment: Build external recognition of your expertise through:

- Professional certifications and continuing education
- Conference presentations and published articles
- Volunteer leadership in professional organizations
- Mentorship and teaching roles
- Network building with other experts

The Scaling Strategy Framework

Moving from individual expertise to scalable income requires systematic progression through increasing levels of leverage:

Phase 1: Direct Monetization (Months 1-6) Start by monetizing your expertise directly through one-on-one or small group interactions:

- Consulting projects for healthcare organizations
- Training delivery for hospital units
- Speaking engagements at conferences
- Specialized per diem or contract work

Phase 2: Systematic Development (Months 6-18) Create reproducible systems and content that can serve larger audiences:

- Standardized training curricula
- Written protocols and procedures
- Online course content
- Group coaching or education programs

Phase 3: Product Creation (Months 12-36) Develop products that generate income without requiring your ongoing time investment:

- Self-paced online courses
- Digital resources and tools
- Subscription-based content
- Licensed methodologies

Phase 4: Business Development (Years 2-5) Build businesses or partnerships that leverage your expertise at scale:

- Educational companies or platforms
- Consulting firms specializing in your expertise area
- Technology companies where you provide subject matter expertise
- Investment opportunities in healthcare ventures

Content Creation and Digital Leverage

The most scalable expertise monetization happens through digital content that can reach unlimited audiences without requiring additional time investment per participant.

Educational Content Development: Transform your clinical knowledge into structured educational content:

- Step-by-step procedure guides
- Case study analysis frameworks
- Decision-making algorithms
- Troubleshooting methodologies

Platform Selection and Optimization: Choose platforms that match your expertise and audience:

- Learning management systems for formal courses
- Video platforms for demonstration content
- Podcast platforms for discussion-based content
- Written platforms for detailed analysis

Content Marketing and Distribution: Develop systematic approaches to reaching your target audience:

- Social media content that demonstrates expertise
- Professional network engagement
- Partnership with healthcare organizations
- Search engine optimization for discoverability

The Network Effect

Your professional network isn't just a source of opportunities—it's a multiplication factor that amplifies the value and reach of your expertise.

Referral Network Development: Build relationships with professionals who can refer opportunities:

- Former colleagues in leadership positions
- Vendors and consultants who work with healthcare organizations
- Other nurse experts in complementary specialties
- Healthcare administrators and decision-makers

Collaboration and Partnership: Create opportunities for mutual benefit with other experts:

- Joint training programs combining different expertise areas
- Cross-referrals for opportunities outside your specialty
- Collaboration on content creation or research projects
- Partnership on larger consulting or implementation projects

Community Building: Establish yourself as a thought leader in your expertise area:

- Facilitate professional discussion groups
- Host educational events or webinars
- Contribute to professional publications
- Mentor other nurses developing similar expertise

Quality and Sustainability Considerations

As you scale your expertise, maintaining quality and managing workload becomes critical for long-term success.

Quality Assurance Systems: Develop processes that ensure consistent value delivery:

- Standardized content development procedures
- Feedback collection and improvement processes
- Continuous education to maintain cutting-edge knowledge
- Peer review and validation of content accuracy

Workload Management: Structure your expertise monetization to enhance rather than compete with your nursing career:

- Batch similar activities to improve efficiency
- Automate administrative and routine tasks
- Set clear boundaries around availability and scope
- Price services appropriately to ensure sustainability

Professional Development Investment: Continue investing in your expertise to maintain competitive advantage:

- Advanced certifications and education
- Conference attendance and networking
- Research and staying current with best practices
- Technology skills that enhance content delivery

The goal isn't to replace your nursing career with expertise monetization—it's to create additional income streams that leverage your professional knowledge while enhancing your overall career satisfaction and financial security.

Wealth Work: Expertise Monetization Assessment

Time needed: 75 minutes

Impact: High - This reveals hidden income opportunities in your existing expertise

Part 1: Expertise Inventory (20 minutes)

Clinical Expertise Assessment: List your areas of specialized knowledge and experience:

Patient Populations:

- Which patient groups do you work with most successfully?
- What age ranges or conditions are you most skilled with?
- Which populations do colleagues ask you about?

Procedures and Technologies:

- What procedures do you perform that others find challenging?
- Which technologies are you known for understanding well?
- What equipment or systems do you troubleshoot for others?

Problem-Solving Specialties:

- What types of clinical problems do colleagues bring to you?
- Which situations do you handle that stress other nurses?
- What processes have you improved or systematized?

Knowledge Areas:

- What topics do you find yourself teaching informally?
- Which protocols or guidelines do you know exceptionally well?
- What continuing education do you pursue actively?

Part 2: Market Demand Analysis (15 minutes)

Problem Identification: For each area of expertise, identify specific problems it solves:

For Other Nurses:

- What questions do colleagues ask you repeatedly?
- Which skills do you see other nurses struggling to develop?
- What knowledge gaps do you notice in your workplace?

For Healthcare Organizations:

- What inefficiencies could your expertise help resolve?
- Which quality or safety issues could your knowledge address?
- What training needs do you observe in healthcare settings?

For Patients and Families:

- What education do you provide that could be systematized?
- Which patient care approaches could be taught to others?
- What communication strategies could benefit more families?

Part 3: Monetization Opportunity Mapping (25 minutes)

Direct Service Opportunities:

Training and Education:
- Hospital units that could benefit from your expertise: _____

_____

- Conference topics you could present: _____
- Online course subjects you could develop: _____

Consulting and Advisory:
- Healthcare organizations that could use your knowledge: _____

_____

- Quality improvement projects where you could contribute: _____

_____

▦ Policy development opportunities in your expertise area: _____

_____

Content Creation:

▦ Written resources (protocols, guides, articles) you could develop: _

_____

▦ Video or multimedia content you could create: _____

_____

▦ Digital tools or apps incorporating your expertise: _____

_____

Product Development:

▦ Educational programs you could license: _____

▦ Certification courses you could create: _____

▦ Subscription content you could develop: _____

Part 4: Competitive Analysis and Positioning (15 minutes)

Existing Solutions Research: For your top expertise area, research what's currently available:

Training Companies:

▦ Who currently provides education in your specialty? _____

_____

▦ What do they charge? _____

▦ What gaps exist in their offerings? _____

Educational Content:

▦ What online courses or resources already exist? _____

▦ How could you provide superior value? _____

▦ What unique perspective do you bring? _____

Professional Positioning:

▦ What makes your expertise unique? _____

- How does your background differ from competitors? _____

  _____

- What credibility factors support your expert positioning? _____

  _____

Part 5: Monetization Strategy Development

Priority Opportunity Selection: Choose your top 3 expertise monetization opportunities:

Opportunity #1: _____

- **Target audience:** _____
- **Problem it solves:** _____
- **Delivery method:** _____
- **Potential income:** $_____per month
- **Time investment required:** _____ hours per month
- **Timeline to launch:** _____ months

Opportunity #2: _____

- **Target audience:** _____
- **Problem it solves:** _____
- **Delivery method:** _____
- **Potential income:** $_____per month
- **Time investment required:** _____ hours per month
- **Timeline to launch:** _____ months

Opportunity #3: _____

- **Target audience:** _____
- **Problem it solves:** _____
- **Delivery method:** _____
- **Potential income:** $_____per month
- **Time investment required:** _____ hours per month
- **Timeline to launch:** _____ months

Part 6: Implementation Planning

First 90 Days Action Plan:

Month 1: Foundation Building ☐ Research pricing for similar services in your expertise area ☐ Create professional bio highlighting your qualifications ☐ Identify 5 potential first customers or opportunities ☐ Develop one-page description of your expertise and services

Month 2: Content Development ☐ Create outline for your first educational offering ☐ Develop sample content (slides, handouts, or materials) ☐ Test content with trusted colleagues for feedback ☐ Refine based on input and finalize first offering

Month 3: Market Testing ☐ Reach out to identified potential customers ☐ Offer first service at introductory rate to build testimonials ☐ Collect detailed feedback on value and improvement opportunities ☐ Begin building portfolio of work samples and testimonials

Success Metrics:

- Number of prospects contacted: _____
- Services delivered: _____
- Revenue generated: $_____
- Customer satisfaction scores: _____
- Referrals received: _____

Part 7: Mindset and Positioning Work

Value Proposition Development: Complete these statements about your expertise:

"I help _____ (target audience) solve _____ (specific problem) through _____ (your unique approach) so they can achieve _____ (desired outcome)."

Pricing Psychology:

- What hourly rate reflects the value you provide? $_____
- How does this compare to what training companies charge? $_____
- What would you pay for expertise that solved a significant problem for you? $_____

Professional Positioning:

- How will you introduce yourself as an expert rather than just a nurse?
- What credentials or experience support your expert positioning?
- How will you communicate your value to potential clients?

Confidence Building: Write down 3 specific examples of times your expertise made a significant difference:

1. _____
2. _____
3. _____

These examples become the foundation for your marketing and positioning as you build expertise-based income streams.

Coming Next: In Chapter 7, Olivia calculates her Freedom Number and realizes that financial independence isn't as far away as she thought. She'll learn how to create a clear timeline for making nursing optional rather than mandatory, and discover why time freedom often makes nurses better at their jobs, not worse.

T - TIME FREEDOM & FINANCIAL INDEPENDENCE

"Financial independence isn't about escaping work, it's about buying back the power to choose your own path."

Olivia's Story

ONCE AGAIN, OLIVIA SAT IN THE HOSPITAL PARKING GARAGE, BUT this time she wasn't crying. She was staring at her phone screen in disbelief, refreshing her investment app for the third time to make sure the numbers were real.

It had been eight months since her conversation with Cara that started this whole transformation. Eight months since she'd realized she was sitting on an abundance of professional assets. Eight months since she'd started investing $400 monthly and building her ECMO consulting business.

The numbers on her screen told a story that seemed impossible: her investment account showed $4,847, her emergency fund had grown to $12,000, and her consulting income this month alone was $3,200. But it was the calculation she'd just finished on her phone's notes app that made her hands shake with excitement.

Freedom Number Calculation:

- Monthly expenses: $5,800
- Annual expenses: $69,600
- Freedom Number (expenses × 25): $1,740,000
- Current total assets: $487,000 (including home equity)
- Monthly wealth building: $1,200 average
- **Time to Freedom: 8.7 years**

Eight years and eight months. That's how long until she could make nursing completely optional.

She'd expected the calculation to show she needed twenty-five or thirty years. Maybe more. The realization that financial independence wasn't some distant dream but an achievable goal within a decade felt like discovering she could fly.

Her phone buzzed with a text from Mickey: *"Madison's at practice for another hour. Want to grab coffee and celebrate your consulting win this month?"*

She typed back: *"Yes, but I have something even bigger to celebrate. Meet you there in 10."*

Shortly after, she slid into the booth across from Mickey at their neighborhood coffee shop, trying to contain her excitement. He looked tired—construction work had been tough this fall—but his eyes lit up when he saw her expression.

"Okay, spill it," he said, grinning. "You look like you just won the lottery."

"I kind of did," Olivia said, pulling out her phone. "But not the kind you're thinking. Mickey, I figured out when we can be financially free."

She showed him the calculation, watching his face change as he processed the numbers.

"Wait," he said slowly. "This is saying that in less than nine years, you could stop working if you wanted to?"

"We could stop working if we wanted to," Olivia corrected. "Your income counts too. But yes, that's exactly what it's saying."

Mickey leaned back in his seat, running his hand through his hair. "Olivia, nine years ago Madison wasn't even born. Nine years from now, she'll be fourteen. We could be... free?"

"Free to choose," Olivia said. "Free to work because we love it, not because we have to. Free to take risks, to advocate without fear, to say no to things that don't align with our values."

She watched Mickey's expression shift from disbelief to wonder to something that looked like relief. They'd never talked explicitly about feeling trapped, but she could see in his eyes that he felt it too—the weight of mandatory work, of bills that demanded overtime, of dreams deferred because survival came first.

"How is this possible?" he asked. "Eight months ago you were crying about our finances."

Olivia thought about everything that had changed. Not just the numbers, but the way she understood money, work, and her own value. "I learned that everything I thought I knew about nurses and wealth was wrong. We're not doomed to struggle forever. We have skills and opportunities I never knew existed."

She pulled up her consulting income spreadsheet. "Look at this. Last month I made more from consulting than from most overtime shifts, and I did it from our couch while Madison watched movies. The month before, I made $2,800 helping hospitals optimize their ECMO protocols. This isn't even my main job—it's just sharing knowledge I already have."

Mickey studied the numbers. "And you're still working full-time at the hospital?"

"For now. But that's the beauty of this plan. I don't have to choose between financial security and nursing. As our wealth grows, I can make nursing decisions based on what I love about the work, not what I need to survive."

She thought about her last shift, how different it had felt knowing she was building toward freedom rather than just paying bills. She'd felt more present with her patients, more willing to advocate with difficult physicians, more like the nurse she'd dreamed of becoming in school.

"There's something else," she said. "I've been thinking about what we could do with real financial freedom. Not just for us, but for other nurses. Madison could go to any college she wants without us going into debt. We could support causes we care about. I could teach other nurses how to build wealth, maybe even start something bigger."

Mickey reached across the table and took her hand. "You're talking about this differently than you talk about work."

"What do you mean?"

"You sound... I don't know, powerful? Like you're planning to change the world instead of just survive it."

Olivia beamed. "Maybe that's what happens when you stop being desperate. When you know you have choices, you start making different ones."

She looked around the coffee shop at the afternoon crowd—nurses from other hospitals on their days off, teachers grading papers, parents juggling laptops and toddlers. How many of them knew they were closer to financial freedom than they thought? How many were trapped by stories about money that weren't even true?

"Mickey," she said suddenly, "what if we documented this journey? What if we showed other people it's possible?"

He smiled. "Now you definitely sound like you're planning to change the world."

"Maybe I am," Olivia said, surprising herself with the conviction in her voice. "Maybe that's what happens when you realize that time freedom isn't just about having choices—it's about having the power to make choices that matter."

As they sat in that coffee shop booth, calculating different scenarios and dreaming about possibilities that had seemed impossible just months before, Olivia understood something profound about financial independence. It wasn't really about the money at all.

It was about becoming the person she was meant to be—the nurse, the mother, the leader who could operate from strength instead of scarcity, from vision instead of survival, from love instead of fear.

And for the first time in her adult life, that person felt not just possible, but inevitable.

TIME FREEDOM & FINANCIAL INDEPENDENCE

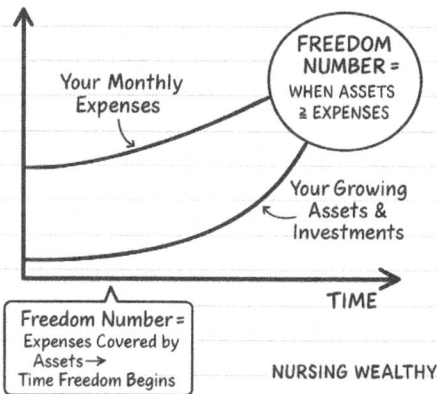

FREEDOM NUMBER = WHEN ASSETS ≥ EXPENSES

Your Monthly Expenses

Your Growing Assets & Investments

TIME

Freedom Number = Expenses Covered by Assets → Time Freedom Begins

NURSING WEALTHY

The Mathematics of Freedom

When I work with nurses who are serious about building wealth, there's always a moment—usually around month six or eight of their transformation—when they experience what I call "The Freedom Calculation." It's the moment Olivia just experienced: realizing that financial independence isn't a distant dream requiring decades of sacrifice, but an achievable goal with a concrete timeline.

This moment is transformational because it fundamentally changes how you think about time, work, and choice. You're probably closer to financial independence than you think.

Understanding Your Freedom Number

Your Freedom Number is the amount of money you need invested to maintain your current lifestyle without working. The standard calculation is simple: multiply your annual expenses by 25. This assumes a 4% withdrawal rate from your investments, which historically allows your money to last indefinitely while maintaining purchasing power.

But for nurses, the calculation needs modification as we have unique advantages that traditional financial independence models don't account for.

The Standard Calculation:

- Annual expenses: $60,000
- Freedom Number: $60,000 × 25 = $1,500,000

The Nursing-Modified Calculation:

- Annual expenses: $60,000
- Minus potential part-time nursing income: -$15,000
- Minus professional stability buffer reduction: -$5,000
- Modified annual need: $40,000
- **Nursing Freedom Number: $40,000 × 25 = $1,000,000**

This difference—$1 million versus $1.5 million—represents years off your timeline to freedom.

Here's why nurses have advantages in reaching financial independence:

Income Flexibility: Your nursing license allows you to generate income even in "retirement" through part-time, casual, or per-diem work, reducing the total amount you need to have fully invested.

Recession-Proof Skills: Economic downturns often increase demand for healthcare services. Your skills become more valuable during the exact conditions that destroy other people's financial independence plans.

Flexible Income Potential: Even in "retirement," you can work when you choose to—picking up shifts during nurse shortages, traveling for premium pay, or consulting at premium rates.

Geographic Flexibility: Nursing licenses are portable, and your skills are in demand globally. If your cost of living increases, you can relocate to areas where your Freedom Number stretches further, or take advantage of currency differences in international markets.

The Psychology of Enough

The most radical transformation in Olivia's story wasn't mathematical—it was psychological. When she realized financial independence was achievable within a decade, her entire relationship with work changed. She wasn't just surviving her nursing career; she was building toward choosing it.

This psychological shift creates what researchers call "psychological safety"—the confidence that comes from having options. And here's what's fascinating: psychological safety actually makes you better at your job.

When people feel secure about their future, they:

- Take more creative risks
- Advocate more strongly for their values
- Focus better on the task at hand
- Experience less decision fatigue
- Show greater resilience under stress

For nurses, this translates directly into better patient care. When you're not worried about losing your job, you advocate more fearlessly. When you're not stressed about bills, you're more present with patients. When you know you have choices, you make decisions based on what's right rather than what's safe.

Timeline Strategies for Healthcare Professionals

Building wealth as a nurse requires different timeline thinking than traditional careers. We have unique accelerators and unique challenges that affect how quickly we can reach financial independence.

The Nurse Wealth Acceleration Timeline:

Years 1-2: Foundation Building
- Establish emergency fund (3-6 months expenses plus $5,000 healthcare professional buffer)

- Maximize employer retirement matching
- Optimize base salary through negotiation or job changes
- Begin systematic investing ($300-500 monthly minimum)
- *Milestone: $15,000-25,000 total assets*

Years 3-5: Expertise Monetization

- Launch first expertise-based income stream
- Increase investment rate to 20%+ of total income
- Optimize taxes through healthcare-specific strategies
- Build professional network for opportunities
- *Milestone: $75,000-125,000 total assets*

Years 6-8: Acceleration Phase

- Multiple income streams producing $1,000+ monthly
- Investment rate at 25-30% of total income
- Real estate or business ownership consideration
- Leadership roles commanding premium compensation
- *Milestone: $200,000-400,000 total assets*

Years 9-12: Independence Approach

- Side income could replace nursing salary if desired
- Investment accounts generating significant annual returns
- Healthcare benefits secured through part-time nursing or spouse
- True choice about work becomes reality
- *Milestone: Freedom Number achieved*

This timeline assumes moderate income growth and consistent investing. Nurses with specialized skills, leadership roles, or successful side businesses often accelerate significantly.

The Difference Between Retirement and Financial Independence

Traditional retirement planning assumes you'll work until 65, then stop completely. Financial independence is different—it's about reaching the point where work becomes optional, regardless of your age.

For nurses, this distinction is crucial because nursing is often more than just a job even if you did just get into it for the money. It can become an identity and a way of serving others. Financial independence doesn't mean you have to stop nursing—it means you get to choose how, when, and why you practice.

What Financial Independence Looks Like for Nurses:

Choice in Practice Settings: Work in the environments that inspire you, not just those that pay the bills. Choose the pediatric ICU over adult ICU because you love working with families, not because it offers better benefits.

Advocacy Without Fear: Speak up for patients, challenge unsafe practices, and advocate for system changes without worrying about job security. Your financial independence makes you unfireable in the ways that matter.

Selective Shifts: Work the shifts that energize you and align with your family life. Take travel assignments for adventure, not necessity. Pick up overtime when it serves your goals, not your survival.

Innovation and Leadership: Start the nonprofit you've dreamed about. Launch the healthcare technology company that could change patient outcomes. Write the book that shares your expertise. Run for office to influence healthcare policy.

Teaching and Mentoring: Share your knowledge through consulting, teaching, or mentoring without needing to maximize every opportunity for income. Choose impact over earnings.

Geographic Freedom: Practice nursing in underserved areas, international settings, or disaster zones because you want to make a difference, not because you need the money.

Financial independence doesn't end your nursing career—it unleashes it.

How Growing Wealth Changes Your Relationship with Work

As Olivia discovered in the coffee shop, building wealth creates a psychological transformation that goes far beyond numbers in bank accounts. When you know you're building toward freedom, every aspect of your work experience changes.

From Scarcity to Abundance Mindset:

- Instead of hoarding opportunities, you share knowledge freely
- Instead of competing with colleagues, you lift others up
- Instead of protecting your position, you take calculated risks
- Instead of accepting mediocrity, you demand excellence

From Reactive to Strategic Decision-Making:

- You choose assignments based on learning opportunities, not just pay
- You invest in education and certifications for growth, not just requirements
- You build relationships for mutual benefit, not just networking
- You plan career moves for long-term impact, not short-term survival

From Individual to Systems Thinking:

- You see how your financial growth can impact your family, community, and profession
- You understand how individual wealth building contributes to systemic change
- You recognize your responsibility to model possibility for other nurses
- You begin thinking about legacy and lasting impact

This evolution from survival to strategic thinking is why financially independent nurses often become leaders in healthcare transformation. They have the security to take risks and the perspective to see beyond immediate needs.

The Compound Effect of Time Freedom

The most powerful aspect of pursuing financial independence as a nurse isn't reaching the final number—it's how the journey changes you along the way. Every month that you build wealth, every dollar that you invest, every new income stream that you create increases your sense of agency and possibility.

This growing sense of empowerment creates what I call "the compound effect of time freedom." As you move toward financial independence, you start making choices from strength rather than desperation. These stronger choices create better outcomes, which accelerate your wealth building, which increases your sense of empowerment, creating an upward spiral of growth and possibility.

Nurses who embrace this compound effect don't just reach financial independence—they become the leaders, innovators, and change-makers that our profession desperately needs. They have the security to challenge systems, the resources to create solutions, and the perspective to think beyond immediate problems.

Your Freedom Number isn't just about having enough money to stop working. It's about having enough power to work from love instead of fear, from vision instead of survival, from purpose instead of desperation.

And when nurses work from that place of empowerment, we don't just change our own lives—we change healthcare for everyone.

Wealth Work: Calculating Your Path to Freedom

Part 1: Your Freedom Number Calculation

Step 1: Calculate Your True Annual Expenses Track your spending for the last 3 months and multiply by 4, or use last year's spending if you have records:

- Housing (mortgage/rent, insurance, taxes, maintenance): $_____
- Transportation (car payments, insurance, gas, maintenance): $_____
- Food and household necessities: $_____
- Insurance (health, life, disability not through employer): $_____
- Debt payments (minimum payments only): $_____
- Personal and discretionary spending: $_____
- **Total Annual Expenses:** $_____

Step 2: Apply Nursing-Specific Adjustments

- Potential part-time nursing income in
  Financial Independence: -$_____
- Professional stability buffer reduction: -$_____
- **Adjusted Annual Need:** $_____

Step 3: Calculate Your Freedom Number

- Adjusted Annual Need × 25 = $_____
- Traditional calculation (no adjustments) × 25 = $_____
- **Potential savings from nursing advantages:** $_____

Part 2: Current Position Assessment

Your Current Assets:

- Cash and emergency funds: $_____
- Retirement accounts: $_____
- Taxable investment accounts: $_____
- Real estate equity: $_____
- Other assets: $_____
- **Total Current Assets:** $_____

Your Wealth Building Rate:

- Monthly retirement contributions: $_____
- Monthly taxable investments: $_____
- Monthly emergency fund building: $_____
- Average monthly side income: $_____
- **Total Monthly Wealth Building:** $_____

Part 3: Timeline Calculation

Basic Timeline Formula: (Freedom Number - Current Assets) ÷ (Monthly Wealth Building × 12) = ____ **years**

Optimistic Timeline (assuming 7% annual investment returns): Use a compound interest calculator with:

- Present value: Current Assets
- Monthly contribution: Monthly Wealth Building
- Interest rate: 7% annually
- Future value: Freedom Number
- **Result:** _____ **years to Financial Independence**

Conservative Timeline (assuming 5% annual investment returns): Same calculation with 5% interest rate: ____ **years to Financial Independence**

Part 4: Acceleration Strategies

Income Optimization Opportunities: Rate each opportunity from 1-10 based on feasibility for your situation:

- _____ Salary negotiation or job change
- _____ Additional certifications for pay increases
- _____ Overtime optimization (strategic, not excessive)
- _____ Consulting or expertise monetization
- _____Teaching or training opportunities
- _____ Legal nurse consulting
- _____ Medical writing or content creation

- ▦ _____ Healthcare technology advising
- ▦ _____ Part-time telehealth work
- ▦ _____ Creating educational products

Expense Optimization Without Lifestyle Sacrifice:

- ▦ Housing cost reduction through relocation or refinancing: $_____/month savings
- ▦ Transportation optimization: $_____/month savings
- ▦ Insurance optimization: $_____/month savings
- ▦ Tax strategy optimization: $_____/month savings
- ▦ **Total potential monthly savings: $_____**

Part 5: Psychological Preparation

Visualization Exercise: Write 2-3 paragraphs describing what your life looks like when you reach financial independence:

- ▦ How do you choose to spend your time?
- ▦ What kind of nursing work do you do, if any?
- ▦ How has your relationship with work changed?
- ▦ What impact are you making that you couldn't make before?

Fear Assessment: What concerns do you have about pursuing financial independence?

1. _____

2. _____

3. _____

For each concern, write a specific plan to address it.

Values Alignment Check: How does financial independence align with your nursing values and purpose?

_____

_____

_____

Next Month's Action: Choose ONE specific step you'll take this month to accelerate your path to Financial Independence.

Coming Next: In Chapter 8, Olivia discovers that building wealth and achieving financial independence is only the beginning. She'll learn how her growing financial empowerment positions her to become a leader in healthcare transformation and create a legacy that extends far beyond her individual success. Most importantly, she'll understand that protecting her health—physical, mental, and financial—becomes the unshakeable foundation for everything else she wants to build.

H

CHAPTER 8

H - HEALTH AS YOUR FOUNDATION

"You can't build lasting wealth on a foundation of burnout. Your health is your wealth strategy."

Olivia's Story

OLIVIA STOOD IN THE BREAK ROOM AT 3 AM, STARING AT HER reflection in the microwave door. The woman looking back at her had dark circles under her eyes despite getting seven hours of sleep the night before. Her shoulders ached from hunching over patients, her feet throbbed in her supposedly supportive shoes, and she'd already had three cups of coffee just to feel human.

It had been ten months since her financial transformation began, and the numbers were incredible. Her investment account had grown to nearly $6,000, her consulting income was consistently hitting $3,000 per month, and her Freedom Number calculation showed she was ahead of schedule for financial independence. But tonight, something felt wrong.

She'd picked up an extra shift to cover for Leora, her colleague who'd called in sick for the third time this month. Leora was only 29, but she'd been struggling with migraines that were getting worse, missing more work, and Olivia had overheard her on the phone with her husband about their mounting medical bills and lost income.

"Another double?" asked Ted, the night charge nurse, poking his head into the break room. "Girl, you're going to burn yourself out."

The words felt differently than they had a year ago. Back then, Olivia would have brushed off the concern and powered through. But now, with her new understanding of money and investing, Ted's warning felt like a financial advisor telling her she was about to make a costly mistake.

"Actually," she said, surprising herself, "I think I need to go home after this shift."

Ted raised an eyebrow. "The old Olivia would have taken the overtime."

"The new Olivia knows better," she said, though she wasn't entirely sure what she meant.

She finished her shift at 7 AM and drove home through the morning traffic, her mind racing. Instead of feeling victorious about declining extra money, she felt unsettled. Something Cara had said months ago kept echoing in her head: "Your health is your most valuable asset. You can't build wealth if you can't work."

At home, she found Mickey making breakfast for Madison, who was getting ready for school. He looked up when she walked in, and his expression shifted to concern.

"You look exhausted," he said. "Wasn't this supposed to be a regular shift?"

"It was, but Leora called in sick again, and…" Olivia trailed off, realizing she was about to justify why she'd almost stayed for a double despite not needing the money anymore.

Madison looked up from her cereal. "Mommy, are you sick too?"

The innocent question was like a diagnosis she hadn't seen coming. *Am I sick too?*

She thought about the past few weeks. The persistent fatigue that coffee couldn't fix. The way her back ached even on days off. The tension headaches that had become so routine she'd stopped mentioning them.

The way she'd been snapping at Mickey over small things, then feeling guilty about it.

Most concerning was how her decision-making had been affected. Last week, she'd almost made a major investment decision while exhausted after a difficult shift. She'd caught herself just in time, but it made her realize how fatigue was clouding her judgment about money—the very area where she'd been making such smart choices.

"No, sweetheart, I'm not sick," she told Madison. "But I think Mommy needs to take better care of herself."

After Madison left for school, Olivia sat at her kitchen table with her laptop, but instead of checking her investment accounts or working on her consulting business, she found herself researching something else: the health statistics for nurses.

What she found was alarming:

- Nurses have higher rates of back injuries than construction workers
- 70% of nurses report chronic fatigue
- Nurses have twice the rate of depression compared to the general population
- The average nurse retires earlier than planned due to health issues
- Nurses have higher rates of heart disease, diabetes, and autoimmune disorders

But it was the financial impact data that really caught her attention:

- Lost income from disability: $200,000-400,000 over a career
- Early retirement due to health issues: $500,000+ in lost lifetime earnings
- Nurses miss 50% more work days due to injury and illness than other healthcare workers

Her phone buzzed with a text from Cara: *"Coffee later? I have something important to tell you."*

They met at their usual spot that afternoon. Cara looked different—more relaxed, somehow younger despite being in her mid-thirties.

"You look amazing," Olivia said as Cara slid into the booth. "What's your secret?"

Cara laughed. "That's actually what I wanted to talk to you about. Remember how I was always picking up extra shifts, working 60-70 hours a week as a travel nurse?"

Olivia nodded. Cara's income had always been impressive, but she'd seemed to pay for it with constant exhaustion.

"Well, I had a wake-up call three months ago. I was driving home from a shift and fell asleep at a red light. Just for a few seconds, but it scared me enough to take a hard look at what I was doing to myself."

"What did you do?"

"I calculated the real cost of my overtime addiction," Cara said, pulling out her phone. "Not just the money, but on my health. My waistline was expanding from takeout, I started to get heart palpitations from too much caffeine, and the alcohol I was taking as a downer to get to sleep from time to time started to give me hangovers. There were no deposits left to take out from the health bank of Cara."

Olivia leaned forward. "So you cut back?"

"I cut back, started investing in my health like I was investing in the stock market, and you know what happened? My consulting income doubled when I had the energy to do excellent work. My investment returns improved because I was making decisions with a clear head. My relationships got better. And I am no longer headed for an early grave. In fact, I think I've aged backwards."

Cara leaned forward. "Olivia, I know you've been killing it with your wealth-building strategy, but I can see you're heading toward the same trap I fell into. You're treating your health like an expense instead of an investment."

That evening, Olivia sat down with Mickey and showed him what she'd researched about nurse health statistics and the financial impact of neglecting wellness.

"This is terrifying," he said, studying the numbers. "But also... it explains a lot."

"What do you mean?"

"Remember last month when you were considering that investment in the healthcare REIT? You spent hours researching it when you were exhausted after back-to-back shifts, and you almost made a mistake that would have cost us thousands."

Olivia remembered. She'd been so tired she'd misread the financial statements and nearly invested in a company that was actually losing money.

"And there was that week when you were picking up extra shifts to boost your consulting income, but you were so burned out that you delivered subpar work and almost lost a client."

Mickey was right. In her enthusiasm to build wealth quickly, she'd been undermining her own efforts by neglecting the foundation everything else was built on.

"So what do we do?" she asked.

Mickey smiled. "We treat your health like the investment it is. We make it a line item in our wealth-building strategy, not something we sacrifice for wealth building."

That night, Olivia lay in bed thinking about Leora, who was probably lying awake worrying about medical bills and lost income. She thought about Cara's wake-up call. She thought about Madison asking if she was sick too.

Most of all, she thought about the choice in front of her: she could continue trying to build wealth by pushing her body and mind beyond their limits, or she could build wealth by optimizing her most valuable asset—her health—for long-term performance.

For someone who'd spent months learning to think strategically about money, the choice was obvious.

But knowing what to do and implementing it were two different things. Tomorrow, she would start treating her health with the same systematic approach she'd brought to her finances. Because she'd finally understood you can't build lasting wealth on a foundation of burnout.

Her health wasn't separate from her wealth strategy—it was the foundation that made everything else possible.

The Health-Wealth Connection Nurses Miss

When I work with nurses who are serious about building wealth, there's a pattern I see repeatedly. They'll meticulously track their investments, optimize their tax strategies, and develop multiple income streams— then systematically destroy their earning capacity by neglecting their health.

We're experts at caring for others' health. The problem is that we've been conditioned to view self-care as selfish rather than strategic, and we've never been taught to calculate the financial return on investment of our own wellness.

Here's what every nurse needs to understand: your health is your most valuable financial asset. Everything else—your salary, your investments, your side businesses—depends entirely on your ability to show up consistently with energy, focus, and mental clarity.

The True Cost of Poor Health for Nurses

Let's start with the numbers, you can modify these according to your situation. The financial impact of neglecting your health extends far beyond medical bills:

Direct Health-Related Costs:

- Lost income from sick days beyond paid time off: $200-400 per day
- Lost income from disability leave (partial income replacement): $30,000-50,000 annually
- Reduced overtime capacity: $10,000-25,000 annually
- Early retirement due to health issues: $200,000-500,000 lifetime[3]

Opportunity Costs:

- Poor decision-making when exhausted: Unmeasurable but significant
- Reduced consulting/side business capacity: $5,000-20,000 annually
- Missed career advancement opportunities: $100,000+ lifetime
- Increased spending on convenience (takeout, services): $2,000-5,000 annually

Investment in Prevention:

- Fitness and wellness programs: $500-1,200 annually
- Therapeutic treatments (massage, physiotherapy): $1,000-3,000 annually
- Mental health support: $1,000-5,000 annually (varies by healthcare system)
- Nutrition and supplements: $1,000-2,000 annually
- Quality sleep and ergonomic equipment: $500-2,000 one-time

The pattern is clear: investing $4,000-12,000 annually in preventive health can protect against $50,000-500,000 in losses. The return on investment varies by healthcare system and personal circumstances, but remains substantial globally.

Why Nurses Neglect Their Own Health

Understanding why we do this is crucial to changing the pattern. There are specific reasons nurses struggle with self-care that go beyond the obvious time constraints:

Professional Identity Conflicts: We've been taught that good nurses put patients first, always. This creates guilt around prioritizing our own needs, even when doing so would make us better caregivers.

Hypervigilance Training: Nursing school and clinical practice train us to be constantly alert to others' needs while ignoring our own body signals. We become experts at pushing through fatigue, pain, and stress.

Martyr Complex Reinforcement: Healthcare culture often rewards self-sacrifice and treats exhaustion as a badge of honor rather than a warning sign.

All-or-Nothing Thinking: We often believe that if we can't do health and wellness perfectly, we shouldn't try at all. This leads to cycles of neglect followed by unsustainable extreme measures.

Financial Stress Response: When money is tight, health investments feel like luxuries rather than necessities, creating a cycle where financial stress leads to health neglect, which creates more financial stress.

Energy Conservation Miscalculation: We think we're conserving energy by skipping exercise, eating convenience foods, and avoiding "unnecessary" self-care, but these choices actually deplete our energy reserves.

The Burnout-Poor Decisions Cycle

One of the most overlooked aspects of the health-wealth connection is how physical and mental exhaustion affects financial decision-making. Decision fatigue and chronic stress significantly impair:

Impulse Control: Exhausted brains default to immediate gratification over long-term benefits. This leads to overspending, poor food choices, and shortcuts that cost more money long-term.

Risk Assessment: Fatigue impairs your ability to accurately evaluate risks and opportunities, leading to both overly conservative and dangerously risky financial choices.

Complex Analysis: Tired brains struggle with the multi-variable thinking required for investment decisions, career planning, and business development.

Emotional Regulation: Stress and exhaustion increase emotional spending and reduce patience for the delayed gratification required for wealth building.

This creates a vicious cycle: poor health leads to poor financial decisions, which creates financial stress, which further damages health, which leads to even worse financial decisions.

Breaking this cycle requires treating health improvement as a wealth-building strategy, not a separate goal that competes with financial objectives.

Physical Health as Financial Foundation

For nurses, physical health directly impacts earning capacity in ways that other professions don't experience:

Musculoskeletal Health: Nursing is physically demanding. Back injuries, foot problems, and repetitive strain injuries can end careers prematurely. Investing in preventive care—ergonomic equipment, regular massage, strength training—protects your lifetime earning potential.

Cardiovascular Fitness: Shift work, stress, and irregular eating patterns put nurses at higher risk for heart disease. Cardiovascular health affects energy levels, mental clarity, and longevity—all crucial for long-term wealth building.

Sleep Quality: Shift work disrupts circadian rhythms, but poor sleep affects every aspect of performance. Quality sleep improves decision-making, reduces injury risk, and increases productivity in both clinical work and side businesses.

Nutrition and Energy: Irregular schedules often lead to poor eating habits, which create energy crashes that reduce performance and increase healthcare costs. Strategic nutrition provides consistent energy for both patient care and wealth-building activities.

Injury Prevention: Nursing has one of the highest injury rates of any profession. Proactive physical therapy, proper body mechanics training, and fitness programs that strengthen nursing-specific muscle groups provide massive return on investment through injury prevention.

Mental Health as Wealth Multiplier

Mental health might be even more important than physical health for wealth building, because it affects every decision you make:

Stress Management: Chronic stress impairs memory, reduces creativity, and increases impulsive behavior. Effective stress management techniques—meditation, therapy, hobbies—improve financial decision-making and reduce stress-related spending.

Burnout Prevention: Burnout doesn't just make you miserable; it makes you expensive. Burned-out nurses make more mistakes, take more sick days, change jobs more frequently, and retire earlier. Preventing burnout protects your entire career trajectory.

Cognitive Function: Mental clarity is essential for the complex thinking required in both nursing and wealth building. Protecting cognitive function through stress reduction, quality sleep, and mental stimulation pays dividends throughout your career.

Emotional Intelligence: Managing your own emotions and relating effectively to others is crucial for career advancement, networking, and business development. Mental health support improves these skills.

Resilience Building: Wealth building requires persistence through setbacks. Mental health practices build the psychological resilience needed for long-term financial success.

Creating Nurse-Specific Health Investment Strategies

Generic wellness advice doesn't work for nurses because our schedules, stressors, and physical demands are unique. Here are health investment strategies designed specifically for nursing lifestyles:

Shift-Work Optimized Fitness:

- 20-minute high-intensity workouts that can be done at home
- Bodyweight exercises that target nursing-specific muscle groups
- Stretching routines for before and after shifts
- Walking meetings for consulting calls
- Exercise equipment that works in small spaces

Sleep Optimization for Shift Workers:

- Blackout curtains and white noise machines
- Blue light blocking glasses for pre-sleep screen time
- Pre-sleep magnesium and sleep hygiene protocols
- Split sleep strategies for rotating shifts
- Sleep tracking to optimize rest periods

Nutrition for Irregular Schedules:

- Meal prep strategies that work with 12-hour shifts
- Portable, nutritious snacks for break rooms
- Hydration systems that encourage consistent water intake
- Supplements that support shift work (vitamin D, B-complex, omega-3s)
- Emergency healthy meal services for exhaustion periods

Stress Management for High-Stress Environments:

- 5-minute meditation apps that work during breaks
- Breathing techniques for stressful patient situations
- Professional therapy or counseling
- Peer support groups for nurses
- Hobbies that provide mental escape from healthcare

Preventive Care Specific to Nursing:

- Regular massage or chiropractic care for musculoskeletal health
- Annual physical exams with occupational health focus
- Vision and hearing checks (hospital environments are hard on senses)
- Mental health screenings for burnout and depression
- Ergonomic assessments for workplace setup

The Return on Investment of Health Investment

Let's calculate the return on investment of health spending using real numbers (customize these to your situation):

Investment Example: $8,000 annually in health optimization
- Gym membership: $1,200
- Meal prep service: $2,400
- Massage therapy: $1,800
- Mental health counseling: $2,400
- Supplements and health products: $200

Returns:
- Avoided sick days (5 days at $300/day): $1,500
- Maintained overtime capacity: $15,000
- Improved investment decision-making: $5,000 (conservative estimate)
- Avoided minor injury treatment: $3,000
- Extended career longevity: $100,000+ lifetime value

Annual ROI: $24,500 return on $8,000 investment = 306% return
This beats any investment vehicle available to individual investors.

Building Health into Your Wealth Strategy

The key to success is integrating health investments into your overall wealth-building plan rather than treating them as separate expenses:

Health as Asset Protection: Frame health spending as insurance for your earning capacity rather than optional wellness expenses.

Automate Health Investments: Set up automatic transfers to health savings accounts, gym memberships, and preventive care just like you automate investment contributions.

Track Health ROI: Monitor how health investments affect your energy, productivity, and decision-making quality, not just traditional health metrics.

Plan Health Like Investments: Research health interventions, compare costs and benefits, and make systematic decisions rather than emotional ones.

Include Family Health: Your family's health affects your finances too. Investing in their wellness protects against healthcare costs and ensures you have support systems.

Professional Development Integration: Choose continuing education that improves both your nursing skills and your health knowledge, maximizing the investment.

The Compound Effect of Health and Wealth

The most powerful aspect of treating health as a wealth strategy is the compound effect. Every health improvement creates multiple benefits:

Better sleep → Better decisions → Better investments → More wealth → Less stress → Better sleep

Regular exercise → More energy → Higher productivity → More income → Better equipment → Better workouts

Stress management → Clearer thinking → Better relationships → More opportunities → Reduced anxiety → Better stress management

This creates an upward spiral where health improvements accelerate wealth building, which reduces financial stress, which improves health, which accelerates wealth building even more.

Nurses who understand this connection don't just become wealthy—they become sustainably wealthy, building their success on a foundation that can support long-term growth rather than short-term gains that burn out their most valuable asset.

Your health isn't separate from your wealth strategy. It is your wealth strategy. Every dollar you invest in your physical and mental wellness multiplies your capacity to build lasting financial security while serving others from a position of strength rather than depletion.

The nurses who build the most wealth aren't those who sacrifice everything for money—they're those who optimize everything, including their health, for maximum long-term performance.

Wealth Work: Building Your Health Investment Strategy

Part 1: Health Impact Assessment

Current Health Costs Analysis: Track your health-related expenses over the past 12 months:

- Medical appointments and treatments: $_____
- Medications and supplements: $_____
- Sick days (lost income): $_____
- Convenience spending due to exhaustion: $_____
- Stress-related purchases: $_____
- **Total Health-Related Costs:** $_____

Energy and Performance Tracking: Rate yourself 1-10 over the past month:

- Average energy level during work days: _____/10
- Quality of decision-making when tired: _____/10
- Physical comfort during and after shifts: _____/10
- Mental clarity for financial decisions: _____/10
- Overall life satisfaction: _____/10

Warning Signs Inventory: Check all that apply to you currently:

- ☐ Chronic fatigue that doesn't improve with rest
- ☐ Frequent headaches or tension
- ☐ Back, neck, or joint pain
- ☐ Difficulty sleeping or staying asleep
- ☐ Relying on caffeine to function
- ☐ Emotional eating or irregular meals
- ☐ Irritability with family or colleagues
- ☐ Difficulty concentrating on complex tasks

- ☐ Frequent minor illnesses
- ☐ Feeling overwhelmed by financial decisions

Part 2: Health ROI Calculation

Potential Lost Income from Poor Health:

- Estimated sick days per year × daily income: $_____
- Reduced overtime capacity × hourly rate: $_____
- Poor decision-making costs (estimate): $_____
- Missed opportunities due to low energy: $_____
- **Total Annual Risk:**   **$_____**

Health Investment Budget: Calculate 5-8% of your gross income as your health investment target:

- Gross annual income: $_____
- Health investment target (5-8%): $_____
- Current health spending: $_____
- **Investment gap:**   **$_____**

Priority Health Investments: Rank these from 1-10 based on your greatest needs:

- __ Quality sleep optimization (mattress, environment, routine)
- __ Regular exercise program (gym, equipment, trainer)
- __ Nutrition improvement (meal prep, supplements, consultation)
- __ Stress management (therapy, meditation, hobbies)
- __ Preventive care (massage, chiropractic, regular checkups)
- __ Work environment improvements (ergonomic supports, footwear)
- __ Mental health support (counseling, psychiatric care)
- __ Recovery and rest activities (vacation, spa treatments, breaks)
- __ Social support systems (groups, friends, family time)
- __ Professional development in health areas

Part 3: Implementation Planning

Immediate Health Wins (This Month): Choose 3 low-cost, high-impact changes you can implement immediately:

1. _____

2. _____

3. _____

90-Day Health Investment Plan:
- Month 1 focus: _____
- Month 2 focus: _____
- Month 3 focus: _____

Automation Strategy: Set up automatic systems for health maintenance:
- Automated savings for health investments: $_____/month
- Scheduled preventive appointments: _____
- Recurring healthy meal delivery or prep: _____
- Automatic gym membership or fitness app: _____

Accountability System:
- Health tracking method: _____
- Accountability partner: _____
- Monthly health review date: _____
- Health goals progress check: _____

Part 4: Integration with Wealth Building

Health-Wealth Connection Goals:

1. Energy Goal: How will improved health increase your earning capacity?

_____

2. Decision-Making Goal: How will better health improve your financial choices?

_____

3. Longevity Goal: How will health investments protect your long-term wealth building?

_____

Measurement Strategy: How will you track the ROI of your health investments?

- Energy levels and productivity metrics: _____
- Financial decision quality indicators: _____
- Income and opportunity tracking: _____

Part 5: Mindset Shifts

Reframe Exercise: Write new empowering beliefs about health and wealth:

Old belief: "I can't afford to spend money on health and wellness."
New belief: _____

Old belief: "Taking care of myself is selfish when others need me."
New belief: _____

Old belief: "I'll focus on health after I've built wealth."
New belief: _____

Values Alignment: How does investing in your health align with your nursing values and family priorities?

_____

Legacy Vision: What kind of health legacy do you want to create for yourself and your family through your wealth-building journey?

_____

Next Week's Commitment: Choose ONE specific health investment you'll make this week:

_____

Coming Next: In Chapter 9, Olivia discovers that individual wealth building is just the beginning. She'll learn how to scale her success by building systems and businesses that create lasting impact beyond her personal financial goals. Most importantly, she'll understand how individual transformation can spark systemic change in how nurses approach wealth and career empowerment.

03

ACCELERATION

THE COMPOUND EFFECT - WHEN IT ALL COMES TOGETHER

"Wealth building is about creating systems that amplify
each other until success becomes inevitable."

Olivia's Story

OLIVIA STOOD IN FRONT OF THE MIRROR IN THE HOSPITAL BATH-room, but this time she wasn't checking for exhaustion or stress lines. She was adjusting her blazer before heading to a meeting that would have been unimaginable eighteen months ago.

The metrics of her transformation were undeniable. Her investment accounts now totaled $11,847. Her consulting business had grown to consistently generate $4,000-5,000 monthly, with a waiting list of hospitals wanting her ECMO expertise. She'd negotiated a 0.8 FTE position that gave her Fridays off while maintaining full benefits. Most remarkably, she'd calculated that she was ahead of schedule on her Freedom Number—potentially reaching financial independence in 12 years instead of 15.

But the numbers only told part of the story.

The real transformation was in how she moved through the world. Gone was the desperate nurse who picked up overtime to survive. In her place was a strategic professional who made decisions from abundance rather than scarcity. She carried herself differently, spoke up confidently in meetings, and had started saying no to opportunities that didn't align with her values or goals.

Today's meeting was the ultimate test of that transformation.

Dr. Gwen Best, the Chief Nursing Officer, had requested a private meeting to discuss "strategic initiatives." Olivia suspected she knew what it was about—the nurses' wellness program she'd proposed had been gaining traction, and her reputation as someone who understood both clinical excellence and business strategy had spread throughout the hospital system.

She walked into Dr. Best's office with the same confidence she now brought to investment decisions and consulting calls.

"Olivia, thank you for making time," Dr. Best said, gesturing to the chair across from her desk. "I'll get straight to the point. We're creating a new position—Director of Nurse Wellness and Professional Development—and I'd like you to consider it."

Eighteen months ago, Olivia would have immediately calculated the salary increase and accepted without thinking. Today, she listened carefully as Dr. Best outlined the role: developing programs to address nurse burnout, creating professional development pathways, and working with administration to improve working conditions.

"The salary would be $95,000, plus you'd maintain your clinical time at 0.5 FTE," Dr. Best continued. "It's a unique hybrid role that would let you impact nursing practice while staying connected to patient care."

Olivia felt excitement, but tempered with strategic thinking. "This sounds aligned with work I'm already passionate about. Can you tell me more about the scope of authority and budget for initiatives?"

As Dr. Best described the role, Olivia found herself thinking strategically about two very different paths. The position would increase her total income to approximately $140,000 annually—excellent money by traditional nursing standards. It offered prestige, security, and the chance to create meaningful change within the system.

But there was another voice in her head, one that had grown stronger over the past eighteen months: *What if you went all in on your own thing?*

Her consulting business was already generating $4,000-5,000 monthly with a waiting list of clients. She'd been turning down opportunities because she couldn't handle more while working full-time. What if she could handle them all? What if she could scale beyond just her personal expertise?

The Director role was a ceiling—a very nice ceiling at $140,000. But her own business? That was potentially limitless.

"This is an incredible opportunity," Olivia said carefully, "and I'm honored you thought of me. Could I have until next week to consider it fully? There are some strategic factors I need to think through."

Dr. Best smiled. "Of course. And Olivia? The way you've transformed over the past year—your energy, your leadership, your strategic thinking—that's exactly what we need in this role."

After the meeting, Olivia sat in her car in the parking garage where this whole journey had begun. The contrast wasn't lost on her. Eighteen months ago, she'd cried in this same spot, feeling trapped by circumstances she couldn't control. Today, she was evaluating a leadership opportunity that could accelerate her wealth building while creating positive change for other nurses.

She pulled out her phone and did something that had become automatic: she ran the numbers on both scenarios.

Director Role Scenario:
- Total annual income: $140,000
- Security: High
- Growth potential: Limited to salary increases and system advancement
- Impact: Significant within one hospital system
- Time freedom: Moderate (structured but less clinical demands)
- Ceiling: Clear—this would likely be the highest role available to her

All-In Entrepreneur Scenario:
- Current monthly consulting: $4,000-5,000 (with waitlist)
- Projected scaling potential: $10,000-20,000+ monthly
- Security: Lower initially, but building toward true independence
- Growth potential: Unlimited
- Impact: Potentially massive—could affect thousands of nurses
- Time freedom: Complete control over schedule and choices
- Ceiling: None—limited only by her vision and execution

The Director role was a bird in the hand—prestigious, well-paid, meaningful work within a system that valued her. Going all-in on her business was potentially transformational, but required giving up security for possibility.

She texted Mickey: *"Big news. Can we talk when I get home?"*

Two hours later, they sat at their kitchen table with Madison colouring nearby, discussing the opportunity. But the conversation was different from any they'd had before about work decisions.

"It sounds like an amazing opportunity," Mickey said after she'd explained both options. "But I can see something in your eyes when you talk about the business that I don't see when you talk about the Director role."

"What do you mean?"

"When you describe the Director position, you sound grateful and excited. When you talk about scaling your business, you sound like you're on fire. There's a difference."

Mickey was right. The Director role felt like the smart, safe choice—something the old Olivia would have jumped at without question. But the new Olivia, the one who'd learned to think strategically about wealth and possibility, was drawn to the bigger risk with the bigger potential.

"But $140,000 is incredible money for our family," she said, testing her own commitment to the scarier path.

"Eighteen months ago, that would have been our ceiling," Mickey agreed. "But look what you've built already. What if your ceiling is actually much higher than we ever imagined?"

That evening, Olivia found herself doing something she hadn't done in months: she called Cara not for advice, but to think out loud with someone who understood entrepreneurial risk.

"The Director role is what successful nurses are supposed to want," Olivia said. "Leadership, good salary, making change within the system. Why am I even hesitating?"

"Because you're not the same person who would have seen that as the ultimate goal," Cara replied. "You've tasted what it's like to build something from nothing, to have unlimited income potential, to be truly independent. It's hard to go back to working within someone else's vision of what your career should look like."

"But what if I fail? What if I give up security and can't make it work?"

"Olivia, you've proven you can build a successful consulting business while working full-time with a young child. You think you can't make it work with complete focus and freedom?"

Cara was right, but there was something deeper Olivia was grappling with. The Director role wasn't just about money—it was about respectability, about fitting into the traditional nursing career ladder, about proving she'd "made it" in ways other people would understand and admire.

Going all-in on her business meant betting on herself in a way that might look risky or selfish to others, even if the numbers suggested it was actually the smarter long-term choice.

"There's something else," Olivia said. "If I scale my business the way I think I can, I could eventually help more nurses than I ever could in one Director role. But that feels... big. Maybe too big."

"Or maybe it's exactly the right size for who you're becoming," Cara said gently.

Madison looked up from her colouring. "Mommy, would you still be a nurse?"

"Yes, sweetheart, but I'd also be helping other nurses be happier at work."

Mickey reached across the table and took her hand. "Eighteen months ago, you were crying about feeling trapped. Now you're designing systems to help other people escape the same trap. That's not just wealth building—that's leadership."

That evening, after Madison was in bed, Olivia sat with her laptop and did something that had become her method for big decisions: she wrote out the story of each choice as if she were looking back five years from now.

The Director Story: *Five years later, I'm respected throughout the hospital system as someone who created meaningful change in nurse wellness. I've impacted hundreds of nurses directly and influenced policies that affect thousands more. My salary has grown to $160,000, my family is secure, and I have a pension waiting for me. I helped improve nursing from within the system, and I'm proud of the change I created.*

The Entrepreneur Story: *Five years later, I've built a business that's helped thousands of nurses transform their financial lives. I've created online programs, spoken at national conferences, and built a community of financially empowered nurses who are changing healthcare from positions of strength rather than desperation. My income varies but consistently exceeds $300,000 annually, my time is completely my own, and I've created something that impacts the entire profession. I also employ other nurses and have created jobs for people who share my vision.*

Both stories felt good, but only one made her heart race with excitement.

She opened another browser tab and began researching something she'd been curious about but hadn't had time to explore: what would it actually take to scale her consulting business into something bigger?

The numbers were encouraging. Her current client base was limited by her available time, not by demand. She had requests she was turning down weekly. Her expertise in ECMO was rare enough that she could likely command even higher rates if she could offer more comprehensive services.

But beyond the consulting, she'd been getting questions from nurses about the wealth-building strategies she'd shared informally. What if she created a program specifically for nurses who wanted to replicate her transformation? What if she combined her clinical expertise with her financial education to create something that didn't exist anywhere else?

As she researched and planned, Olivia realized she wasn't just choosing between two jobs. She was choosing between two identities: the successful nurse who worked within existing systems, or the nurse entrepreneur who created new possibilities for herself and others.

She opened her laptop and began researching the Nursing Wealthy Accelerator program that Cara had mentioned months ago, but now with a different perspective. Instead of seeing it as education for her own development, she was curious about it as a model for what she might create.

The program description resonated, but she found herself thinking: *What if I could create something specifically for nurses who want to build wealth while scaling their clinical expertise? What if I combined ECMO consulting with financial coaching? What if I helped nurses become entrepreneurs in their own areas of expertise?*

As she read testimonials from nurses who'd built consulting businesses, negotiated significant salary increases, and achieved financial independence, a light flickered inside of her. Her transformation wasn't just replicable—it was scalable. She could potentially help hundreds or thousands of nurses create the same kind of transformation she'd experienced.

But it would mean betting everything on herself rather than accepting the security of institutional success.

She picked up her phone and called Cara, knowing her friend would understand the magnitude of the choice she was facing.

"I was wondering when you'd call back," Cara answered.

"Cara, I think I'm at a crossroads between playing it safe and betting everything on the vision I'm starting to see for myself." Olivia said.

As they talked, Olivia explained both options—the prestigious Director role with its clear path and good salary, versus the uncertain but potentially unlimited path of scaling her own business.

"It sounds like you're choosing between someone else's version of success and your own," Cara said. "The Director role is what everyone would expect you to want. But what do you actually want?"

The question was like a diagnosis she'd been avoiding. What did she actually want, beyond security and respectability and other people's approval?

"I want to show nurses that we don't have to choose between caring for others and building wealth," she said, the words coming out with surprising clarity. "I want to prove that nurses can be entrepreneurs and business owners and wealthy, and that making money actually makes us better at taking care of people, not worse."

"That sounds like a mission, not a job," Cara said. "And missions don't come with guaranteed salaries and pension plans."

After they hung up for the second time that evening, Olivia sat quietly at her kitchen table, understanding that she was at the same kind of pivotal moment she'd experienced eighteen months ago in the hospital parking garage. Not a moment of desperation this time, but a moment of choice between safety and possibility, between conventional success and the chance to create something entirely new.

The compound effect of her wealth-building strategies hadn't just created financial options—it had created the psychological and financial foundation to take risks that would have been impossible before. She had enough money saved, enough income generated, and enough confidence built to choose possibility over security.

Eighteen months ago, she'd been a good nurse trapped in survival mode, desperate for any improvement in her circumstances. Tonight, she was a good nurse operating from strength, with the luxury of choosing between two excellent options based on vision rather than need.

But more than that, she was starting to see herself as someone who could create entirely new categories of success for nurses—someone who could show that the traditional either/or choice between caring and wealth-building was a false dilemma.

The compound effect wasn't just about her investment returns or consulting income. It was about how each element of her transformation had created the foundation for choices she'd never imagined possible.

As she prepared for bed, Olivia felt a mix of excitement and uncertainty that had marked every major breakthrough in her journey.

The revolution that had started with her own financial transformation was ready to scale—if she was brave enough to bet everything on the vision she was only beginning to see.

The Science of Success Acceleration

When I work with nurses who've been implementing wealth-building strategies, I consistently see what Olivia experienced: a point where individual improvements begin creating exponential rather than linear returns. This is the compound effect in action—not just in investment accounts, but across every aspect of their professional and personal lives.

Understanding how this acceleration happens helps you recognize when you're approaching this inflection point and how to maximize its impact.

The Synergy of the WEALTH System

The power of the WEALTH framework isn't in any single element—it's in how each component amplifies the others when implemented together:

Wealth Mindset amplifies everything else:

- Makes you more likely to invest in energy management tools
- Helps you see health expenses as investments rather than costs
- Increases confidence to monetize your expertise
- Supports long-term thinking in all areas

Energy Management multiplies earning capacity:

- Better decisions about investments when well-rested
- More capacity for side business development
- Improved clinical performance leading to advancement opportunities
- Sustainable practices that prevent burnout-related financial setbacks

Asset Building creates psychological safety:

- Reduces financial stress that was draining mental energy
- Provides cushion for taking calculated career risks
- Generates passive income that supports other wealth-building activities
- Builds confidence that compounds across all life areas

Leverage and Expertise Monetization accelerates everything:

- Additional income funds larger investment contributions
- Professional recognition creates advancement opportunities
- Network expansion leads to new business possibilities
- Expertise development makes you more valuable in your primary role

Time Freedom changes your entire relationship with work:

- Ability to be selective about opportunities
- Reduced desperation leading to better negotiation outcomes
- Mental space for strategic thinking about career and investments
- Position of strength in all professional interactions

Health as Foundation supports all other activities:

- Physical energy for wealth-building activities
- Mental clarity for complex financial decisions
- Emotional resilience for long-term goal pursuit
- Longevity to enjoy the wealth you're building

The Momentum Effect

Once these elements begin working together, nurses experience what I call "momentum effect"—where each success makes the next success more likely and more impactful.

Financial Momentum: Early investment gains create confidence for larger contributions. Consulting income provides capital for better investment opportunities. Emergency fund eliminates crisis-driven spending, freeing up money for wealth building.

Professional Momentum: Energy management leads to better work performance. Better performance creates advancement opportunities. Leadership roles provide platforms for expertise monetization. Recognition attracts more lucrative opportunities.

Personal Momentum: Reduced financial stress improves relationships. Better health supports sustained effort. Increased confidence leads to bigger goals. Achievement of goals builds belief in continued possibility.

System Momentum: Automated savings creates wealth without ongoing decisions. Established consulting business generates income with less active effort. Professional reputation creates opportunities without active pursuit. Health habits maintain energy without constant willpower.

Common Acceleration Patterns

While every nurse's journey is unique, I see predictable patterns in how the compound effect manifests:

Months 1-6: Foundation Building Individual strategies begin working. Small wins create confidence. Systems start forming. Energy improves noticeably.

Months 6-12: Integration Phase Strategies begin reinforcing each other. Financial stress decreases meaningfully. Professional confidence increases. Others begin noticing changes.

Months 12-18: Acceleration Point Compound effects become obvious. Multiple opportunities arise simultaneously. Leadership qualities emerge. Impact extends beyond personal transformation.

Months 18+: Scale and Impact Phase Success becomes sustainable and systematic. Focus shifts from personal transformation to helping others. Legacy and leadership thinking emerges. Systemic change becomes possible.

Why Some Nurses Plateau (And How to Break Through)

Not every nurse who starts wealth building reaches the acceleration phase. Understanding common plateau points helps you recognize and overcome them:

The Knowledge Plateau: Problem: Consuming information without implementation **Solution:** Focus on mastering one strategy completely before adding others. Action beats analysis.

The Perfectionism Plateau: Problem: Waiting for perfect conditions to take bigger steps **Solution:** Embrace "good enough" execution over perfect planning. Progress beats perfection.

The Comfort Zone Plateau: Problem: Success in early stages creates complacency **Solution:** Regularly increase targets and challenges. Comfort is the enemy of growth.

The Isolation Plateau: Problem: Trying to sustain transformation without community support **Solution:** Connect with other nurses on similar journeys. Transformation accelerates in community.

The Identity Plateau: Problem: Old self-concept conflicts with new possibilities **Solution:** Regularly update your identity story to match your growing capabilities.

Strategies for Sustained Acceleration

Once you recognize the compound effect beginning in your life, specific strategies can amplify and sustain the momentum:

Double Down on What's Working: Instead of adding new strategies, intensify successful ones. If consulting is working, can you double your capacity? If investments are growing, can you increase contributions?

Leverage Success for More Success: Use achievements as platforms for bigger opportunities. Professional recognition becomes speaking opportunities. Investment knowledge becomes financial coaching. Leadership experience becomes advancement possibilities.

Create Positive Feedback Loops: Design systems where success automatically creates conditions for more success. Investment gains fund larger investments. Consulting income pays for professional development. Recognition attracts better opportunities.

Expand Your Identity: Consciously evolve from someone who "is trying to build wealth" to someone who "is wealthy and building more." Identity drives behavior, which drives results.

Build Anti-Fragile Systems: Create wealth-building systems that get stronger under stress rather than weaker. Multiple income streams, diversified investments, strong health habits, and robust professional networks all provide resilience.

The Ripple Effect: When Personal Transformation Becomes Systemic Change

The most powerful aspect of the compound effect is how individual transformation naturally extends beyond the person who initiated it:

Family Impact: Children observe and internalize wealth-building behaviors. Spouses become more financially strategic. Extended family seeks advice and guidance. Financial security improves relationships across the board.

Professional Impact: Colleagues notice increased confidence and competence. Management recognizes leadership potential. Patients benefit from nurses operating from strength rather than stress. Workplace culture improves through example.

Community Impact: Other nurses seek mentorship and guidance. Professional organizations benefit from leadership contributions. Healthcare systems improve through innovative thinking. The profession advances through individual excellence.

Systemic Impact: Traditional beliefs about nurses and money begin shifting. New possibilities become visible to others. Cultural change happens one transformed nurse at a time. The entire profession elevates through accumulated individual transformations.

Recognizing Your Acceleration Point

How do you know when you've reached the compound effect phase? Look for these indicators:

Financial Indicators:

- Net worth growing faster than contributions alone would explain
- Multiple income streams developing organically
- Investment decisions feeling natural rather than stressful
- Financial goals accelerating ahead of original timelines

Professional Indicators:

- Opportunities seeking you out rather than you seeking them
- Colleagues asking for your advice and mentorship
- Increased confidence in negotiations and career decisions
- Recognition extending beyond your immediate work environment

Personal Indicators:

- Decision-making from abundance rather than scarcity
- Energy levels sustained without constant effort
- Relationships improving across all areas of life
- Future planning feeling exciting rather than overwhelming

Impact Indicators:

- Others implementing strategies you've shared
- Requests for guidance from other nurses
- Invitations to speak or teach about your experience
- Opportunities to create systemic change in your workplace

The Leadership Transition

The compound effect inevitably leads to a crucial transition: from focusing on your own transformation to helping others achieve theirs. This isn't an obligation—it's a natural evolution that occurs when individual success creates capacity for broader impact.

Signs you're ready for this transition include:
- Your own systems running smoothly with minimal ongoing effort
- Regular requests for advice from colleagues
- Desire to create change beyond your individual circumstances
- Recognition of how your success could be replicated by others

This transition often involves:
- Formal leadership roles that utilize your transformation experience
- Teaching or mentoring opportunities
- Business development that scales your expertise
- Community involvement in nursing professional development

Maximizing Long-Term Compound Growth

To ensure the compound effect continues accelerating rather than plateauing:

Continuously Raise Your Standards: What felt like big goals 18 months ago should feel achievable now. Regularly increase your targets to match your growing capabilities.

Invest in Advanced Development: Basic strategies got you to this point. Advanced strategies—coaching programs, masterminds, specialized education—will take you to the next level.

Build Strategic Relationships: Network with other successful nurses, healthcare leaders, and professionals outside nursing. Your network becomes your net worth.

Think in Systems, Not Goals: Focus on building systems that generate ongoing results rather than achieving one-time targets. Systems create lasting change.

Measure What Matters: Track not just financial metrics but energy levels, relationship quality, professional satisfaction, and impact on others. Wealth building is about whole-life optimization.

The compound effect isn't an accident—it's the predictable result of implementing interconnected strategies consistently over time. When you understand how each element of wealth building amplifies the others, you can consciously create conditions for exponential rather than linear growth.

Your individual transformation becomes the foundation for impact that extends far beyond your own life, creating positive change that ripples through your family, profession, and community.

Wealth Work: Accelerating Your Compound Effect

Part 1: Transformation Assessment

Progress Metrics Review: Compare your current situation to 12-18 months ago:

Financial Progress:

- Net worth then: $_____ | Net worth now: $_____
- Monthly investing then: $_____ | Monthly investing now: $____
- Side income then: $_____ | Side income now: $_____
- Emergency fund then: $_____ | Emergency fund now: $____

Professional Progress:

- Position/title then: _____ | Position/title now: _____
- Confidence level (1-10) then: _____ | Confidence level now: _____
- Leadership opportunities then: _____ | Leadership opportunities now: _____
- Professional recognition then: _____ | Professional recognition now: _____

Personal Progress:

- Energy level (1-10) then: _____ | Energy level now: _____
- Health habits then: _____ | Health habits now: _____
- Relationship quality then: _____ | Relationship quality now: _____
- Future optimism (1-10) then: _____ | Future optimism now: _____

Impact Progress:

- Colleagues seeking advice then: _____ | Colleagues seeking advice now: _____
- Mentoring opportunities then: _____ | Mentoring opportunities now: _____
- Speaking/teaching requests then: _____ | Speaking/teaching requests now: _____

Part 2: Compound Effect Analysis

Synergy Identification: For each pair of WEALTH elements, describe how they amplify each other in your life:

Wealth Mindset + Energy Management: How has thinking abundantly improved your energy choices?

_____

Energy Management + Asset Building: How has better energy management accelerated your investing?

_____

Asset Building + Leverage/Expertise: How has financial security enabled expertise monetization?

_____

Leverage + Time Freedom: How has additional income created more choices?

_____

Time Freedom + Health: How has reduced desperation improved your self-care?

_____

Health + Wealth Mindset: How has better health strengthened your abundance thinking?

_____

Part 3: Acceleration Opportunities

Current Success Amplification: Identify your top 3 strategies that are working well and how you could intensify them:

1. Working Strategy: _____

How to Double Down: _____

2. Working Strategy: _____

How to Double Down: _____

3. Working Strategy: _____

How to Double Down: _____

Plateau Assessment: Check any areas where you feel stuck:

- ☐ Knowledge without action (consuming content but not implementing)
- ☐ Perfectionism preventing progress
- ☐ Comfort zone preventing bigger steps
- ☐ Isolation from other growth-minded nurses
- ☐ Old identity conflicting with new possibilities

Breakthrough Strategy: For your biggest plateau area, write a specific plan to break through:

_____

Part 4: Ripple Effect Planning

Current Impact Assessment:

- How many colleagues have asked for your advice in the past 3 months? _____

- What changes have family members made based on your example?

_____

- How has your transformation affected your workplace culture?

_____

Expanded Impact Vision:

- What would you teach other nurses if you had a platform?

_____

- How could your success story help change nursing culture?

_____

- What systems could you create to help other nurses transform?

_____

Leadership Readiness: Rate yourself 1-10 on readiness for:
- Formal mentoring role: _____
- Speaking about your transformation: _____
- Teaching wealth-building strategies: _____
- Creating programs for other nurses: _____

Part 5: Next-Level Development

Advanced Growth Opportunities: Which would most accelerate your continued development?
- ☐ Intensive coaching program (like Nursing Wealthy Accelerator)
- ☐ Mastermind with other successful nurses
- ☐ Advanced business or financial education
- ☐ Leadership development program
- ☐ Speaking/teaching training

90-Day Acceleration Plan: Choose ONE major initiative to implement in the next 90 days:

_____

_____

_____

_____

Accountability Structure:
- Who will support your continued growth? _____
- How will you measure progress? _____
- When will you evaluate and adjust your strategy? _____

Legacy Vision: Complete this statement: "In 5 years, I want to be known as the nurse who..."

Immediate Next Step: What is the single most important action you'll take this week to accelerate your compound effect?

Coming Next: In the next chapter, you'll see how Olivia's transforms not just her wealth, but her entire approach to expertise monetization and knowledge sharing. You'll discover how individual nurses building scalable businesses create systemic change in healthcare, and why the future of nursing includes entrepreneurship as a standard career path, not an exception.

UNLOCK YOUR BONUS RESOURCES

Scan to access your exclusive webinar on building financial freedom in nursing, plus downloadable tools and templates at

www.maryghazarian.com/nursingwealthy

CHAPTER 10

ACCELERATOR ADVANCED: BUILDING YOUR DIGITAL EMPIRE

"The difference between a nurse who consults and a nurse who builds wealth is the difference between trading time for money and creating assets that generate income while you sleep."

Olivia's Story

OLIVIA STARED AT HER LAPTOP SCREEN, FEELING SIMULTANEOUSLY excited and overwhelmed. She was three months into the Nursing Wealthy Accelerator program, and today's mastermind session had just blown her mind. Around her virtual conference room were twelve other nurses, each at different stages of building businesses that would have seemed impossible just years ago.

Sarah from Toronto had just shared her quarterly revenue: $63,000 from her perimenopause coaching program—running three cohorts every quarter. Josh from Denver was launching his third cohort of "Trauma-Informed Leadership for Healthcare Managers" and had a waitlist of 200 people. Deedee had built a digital course for new NICU nurses that was generating $15,000 monthly in passive income.

And then there was Olivia, still doing mostly 1:1 ECMO consulting, making good money—$6,000-8,000 monthly—but feeling like she was missing something bigger.

"Olivia," said the familiar voice of Martina, who was facilitating today's session as one of the Accelerator's lead coaches. "I can see you're processing. What's coming up for you?"

"I'm grateful for where I am," Olivia began carefully. "The consulting is going well, I'm helping hospitals improve their ECMO programs, and the income has transformed my family's life. But listening to everyone else... I feel like I'm still trading time for money. Like I'm just a really well-paid employee of multiple hospitals instead of building something that could scale."

Martina smiled knowingly. "Perfect awareness. That's exactly the transition we want to help you make. You've mastered the fundamentals—you're financially secure, you've proven your expertise has market value, and you've built systems that work. Now we're ready to help you build assets, not just income streams."

Olivia knew she'd been thinking like a consultant—her time for their money. But the other nurses in the program had moved beyond that. They'd created products, programs, and systems that generated revenue whether they were actively working or not.

"Let's workshop this together," Martina continued. "Olivia, you're the go-to ECMO expert for hospitals across three provinces. You've successfully consulted on over 200 cases in the past 18 months. What if instead of teaching one hospital at a time, you could teach hundreds of nurses simultaneously?"

Ideas started swirling in Olivia's mind, but her perfectionist tendencies were also triggered. "I wouldn't even know where to start. Creating an online program seems so... complicated. And what if it's not as effective as 1:1 consulting?"

"Sarah, remember when you felt exactly the same way about your perimenopause program?" Martina asked.

Sarah laughed from her square on the screen. "Oh god, yes. I was convinced no one would pay for a group program when they could get individual coaching. I was so wrong. The group dynamic actually makes the transformation more powerful, not less. And instead of helping 20 women per year individually, I'm helping 300+ through my programs."

"Tell Olivia your numbers," Martina encouraged.

"My program is called 'The Clarity Code: Menopause Mastery for High-Performing Women,'" Sarah explained. "It's a 6-week group coaching program priced at $897. I run it six times per year with 20-30 women per cohort. Last quarter I generated $63,000 in twelve weeks across three cohorts, and now I have women asking me to create an advanced program."

Olivia felt inspired. "So instead of teaching ECMO one-on-one to individual hospitals, I could create a comprehensive program that teaches critical care nurses everything they need to know about ECMO management?"

"Exactly!" Martina said. "But let's get specific. What would that look like?"

Over the next hour, the group helped Olivia brainstorm what became the foundation of her digital empire:

Program Name: "ICU Mastery Academy: Critical Care Confidence for New Nurses"

Target Audience: New ICU nurses in their first 2 years, who feel overwhelmed and under-prepared for complex cases like ECMO

Problem They're Solving: New ICU nurses are terrified of ECMO patients, often feel inadequate, and worry they'll make life-threatening mistakes

Program Structure:
- 8-week live group coaching program
- Weekly 90-minute sessions combining education and case study analysis

- Private online group for ongoing support
- Resource library with protocols, checklists, and troubleshooting guides
- Certificate of completion for continuing education credits

Pricing Strategy: $997 per person (positioning as professional development investment)

Revenue Potential: 25 nurses per cohort × $997 = $24,925 per launch, with 4-5 launches per year

"Wait," Olivia said, doing quick math in her head. "That's potentially $100,000-125,000 annually from one program? While still maintaining my consulting work?"

"Now you're thinking like a CEO," Martina replied. "But here's the best part—once you create the curriculum and establish the format, your cost per additional student is essentially zero. You can scale from 10 students to 100 students without proportionally increasing your workload."

Josh chimed in from Denver: "Olivia, that's exactly what happened with my leadership program. My first cohort was 8 people at $997 and I made $8,000. My most recent cohort was 35 people at $1,497 and I made $52,395. Same time investment, more impact, significantly more income."

But Olivia's analytical mind was already identifying challenges. "What about the technology? The marketing? The legal stuff? I know ECMO inside and out, but I don't know anything about building online programs."

"That's why you're in the Accelerator," Martina said. "We don't just teach you business theory—we help you implement. Sarah, tell Olivia about your launch process."

Sarah shared her screen, showing a sophisticated but manageable system: "I use ConvertKit for email marketing, Kajabi for hosting the program content, Zoom for live sessions, and Stripe for payments. But I didn't build this overnight. The Accelerator gave me templates, step-by-step guides, and most importantly, support when I got stuck."

"Plus," added Deedee, "you don't have to figure out marketing from scratch. The Accelerator teaches you exactly how to position your expertise, create compelling content, and attract your ideal students. I went from zero email subscribers to 5,000 in eight months using their strategies."

Olivia nodded. "Here's what we're going to do, Olivia. Over the next 90 days, we're going to help you build and launch your first cohort of the ICU Mastery Academy. Not someday—in 90 days."

Olivia felt her stomach flip with excitement and terror. "That feels impossibly fast."

"It's not," Martina assured her. "You already have the expertise. You already have the credibility. You already have hospitals asking for your help. We're just going to help you package that expertise into a scalable format and find the right students."

The group spent the remaining session outlining Olivia's 90-day launch plan:

Days 1-30: Content Creation and Platform Setup
- Outline curriculum based on most common ECMO challenges
- Set up Kajabi platform and payment processing
- Create lead magnet: "ECMO Quick Reference Guide for ICU Nurses"
- Begin building email list through nursing networks

Days 31-60: Marketing and Pre-Launch
- Create content showcasing ECMO expertise on LinkedIn
- Share success stories from previous consulting clients
- Build waitlist through free masterclass: "The 5 Critical ECMO Mistakes That Every ICU Nurse Makes"
- Partner with nursing education companies for cross-promotion

Days 61-90: Launch and Delivery

- Open enrollment for first cohort
- Goal: 15-20 students for pilot program
- Begin program delivery while gathering testimonials
- Plan improvements for next cohort

"This is feeling real," Olivia said, her excitement overriding her nervousness. "But what if only 5 people sign up? What if I'm not good at group teaching? What if—"

"Olivia," Martina interrupted gently, "you're thinking like someone who's never succeeded at anything. But you have succeeded. You built a consulting business from nothing. You've helped hundreds of patients through ECMO procedures. You've transformed your own financial life. Why would this be different?"

Deedee added, "My first program launched with 8 people. I was convinced it was a failure. But those 8 people got incredible results, gave me amazing testimonials, and told their colleagues. My second cohort had 22 people. My third had 45. Success builds on success."

As the session ended, Olivia felt the same mix of excitement and determination she'd felt when she first started investing, when she launched her consulting practice, when she calculated her Freedom Number. The Accelerator wasn't just teaching her business skills; it was expanding her vision of what was possible.

That evening, she called Mickey to debrief from the session.

"So let me get this straight," he said after she'd explained the program concept. "Instead of teaching one hospital's nurses about ECMO for $3,000, you could teach 25 nurses from different hospitals for $25,000?"

"Exactly. And those 25 nurses will then go help thousands of patients, spreading the knowledge much further than I could reach individually."

"And this is in addition to your consulting work, not instead of it?"

"Right. The consulting proves my expertise and gives me case studies. The program scales that expertise to help more people."

Mickey was quiet for a moment. "Olivia, two years ago you were working overtime to pay bills. Now you're talking about building a business that could generate six figures annually while helping nurses across the country. Do you realize how incredible that is?"

She did realize it, but it was still surreal. The Accelerator had shown her that the difference between successful nurse entrepreneurs and those who stayed stuck wasn't talent or luck—it was having the right frameworks, community support, and strategic guidance.

As she started outlining her curriculum that night, Olivia understood she was at another pivotal moment. Not just in her own wealth-building journey, but in her capacity to influence the nursing profession. The program she was creating wouldn't just generate income—it would potentially save lives by making ICU nurses more confident and competent with complex cases.

The revolution that had started with her own financial transformation was about to scale in ways she'd never imagined.

From Time-Trading to Empire Building

What Olivia experienced in that Accelerator session represents the most crucial transition in professional wealth building: moving from trading time for money to creating scalable assets that generate income without constant personal input. This shift is what separates nurses who build comfortable side incomes from those who build true wealth and lasting impact.

The Consulting Trap That Keeps Nurses Small

Most nurses who successfully monetize their expertise get stuck in what I call the "golden handcuffs of consulting." They're making good money—often excellent money—but they're still fundamentally trading hours for dollars. Even at premium rates, this model has built-in limitations:

Time Constraints: There are only so many hours in a week, even at high hourly rates. A nurse charging \$200/hour is still capped by available time.

Client Dependency: Income stops when you stop working. Every month requires starting over with client acquisition and delivery.

Scaling Limitations: Growing income requires proportionally increasing work hours or constantly finding higher-paying clients.

Burnout Risk: The pressure to always be "on" and available can recreate the same stress patterns that nurses are trying to escape.

No Exit Strategy: When you stop consulting, the income stops immediately. There's no asset to sell or passive income stream to maintain.

This is why the Accelerator focuses on transitioning successful consultants to scalable business models. Rather than abandoning consulting, we want to use consulting success as the foundation for building assets that compound over time.

The Digital Leverage Revolution

Digital programs and online education represent the ultimate leverage for nursing expertise. When you create a digital program, you're essentially packaging your knowledge into a format that can serve hundreds or thousands of people simultaneously, without requiring proportional increases in your time investment.

The Mathematics of Digital Leverage:

Traditional Consulting Model:

- 1 nurse consultant + 1 client = \$200/hour
- Maximum monthly income: \$200 × 160 hours = \$32,000 (unsustainable)
- Growth requires more hours or constant client replacement

Digital Program Model:

- 1 nurse expert + 25 students = $997 × 25 = $24,925 per cohort
- Same expert delivers to 50 students = $997 × 50 = $49,850 per cohort
- Same expert delivers to 100 students = $997 × 100 = $99,700 per cohort
- Growth happens through marketing and reputation, not additional hours

The Compound Effect of Scalable Programs:

Unlike consulting, digital programs compound in multiple ways:

Knowledge Compound: Each cohort teaches you how to improve delivery, leading to better outcomes and higher prices over time.

Reputation Compound: Success stories from program graduates create marketing material and referrals for future cohorts.

Community Compound: Program alumni become advocates, affiliate partners, and sources of advanced program ideas.

Content Compound: Material created for programs can be repurposed into books, speaking engagements, and additional revenue streams.

Network Compound: Teaching programs positions you as a thought leader, creating opportunities beyond the program itself.

The Accelerator Advantage: Why Community Matters

What makes the Nursing Wealthy Accelerator different from generic business courses is the combination of nurse-specific expertise and peer community support. As Olivia experienced, having other nurses who've successfully made the transition provides both practical guidance and psychological support for what can feel like an overwhelming shift.

Peer Learning Acceleration: When Sarah shared her perimenopause program results, Olivia didn't just learn about revenue potential—she saw proof that the model worked for healthcare professionals. This peer validation is crucial for overcoming the imposter syndrome that keeps many nurses from scaling their impact.

Industry-Specific Strategies: Generic business coaching might teach program creation, but it won't understand the unique challenges of marketing to nurses, navigating healthcare regulations, or positioning clinical expertise in educational formats. The Accelerator provides frameworks developed specifically for healthcare professionals.

Accountability and Support: Building a scalable business requires sustained effort over months, not days. The community aspect of the Accelerator provides accountability, troubleshooting support, and encouragement during the inevitable challenges of program creation and launch.

Advanced Strategy Access: As Olivia discovered, the Accelerator doesn't just teach basic business principles—it provides advanced strategies like pricing psychology, launch sequences, and scaling frameworks that most entrepreneurs figure out through expensive trial and error.

The Program Creation Framework

The systematic approach the Accelerator uses for helping nurses create successful programs follows a proven methodology:

Step 1: Expertise Audit Identify your unique clinical knowledge and the specific problems it solves. Olivia's ECMO expertise solving the problem of new ICU nurses feeling unprepared for complex cases.

Step 2: Market Validation Confirm that people are actively seeking solutions to the problems you can solve. This often comes from consulting experience—if hospitals are paying you individually, nurses will pay for group education.

Step 3: Curriculum Development Structure your knowledge into a logical learning progression that creates transformation, not just information transfer. The key is focusing on outcomes, not just content.

Step 4: Program Positioning Price and position your program based on the transformation value, not the hours of content. Professional development for nurses should be priced as an investment in career advancement, not consumed as entertainment.

Step 5: Technology Setup Implement simple but professional systems for content delivery, payment processing, and student communication. The goal is functionality, not perfection.

Step 6: Marketing and Launch Use content marketing and professional networks to attract ideal students. Healthcare professionals respond to credibility and peer recommendations more than typical marketing tactics.

Step 7: Delivery and Optimization Focus on student results in your first cohort, gathering testimonials and feedback for improvement. Each iteration should be better than the last.

Advanced Revenue Models Beyond Basic Programs

Once nurses master the basic program model, the Accelerator introduces advanced revenue strategies that create multiple income streams from the same expertise:

Certification Programs: Create ongoing revenue through trainer certifications and licensing your methodology to other experts.

Corporate Training: Scale individual programs into corporate contracts with hospital systems and healthcare organizations.

Advanced Cohorts: Develop higher-level programs for graduates of your basic program, creating a natural progression and increased lifetime customer value.

Done-With-You Services: Combine group education with individual implementation support at premium pricing.

Digital Products: Create templates, checklists, and tools that generate passive income between program launches.

Speaking and Events: Use program success to book keynote speaking engagements and workshop facilitation.

Book and Media Opportunities: Program content becomes the foundation for books, podcasts, and media appearances that expand your platform.

The Psychology of Scaling Impact

One of the most significant shifts nurses experience when transitioning from consulting to programs is psychological. Moving from helping one person at a time to helping hundreds simultaneously requires expanding your sense of identity and impact.

From Helper to Leader: Instead of being the nurse who solves problems individually, you become the nurse who empowers others to solve problems themselves.

From Perfect Execution to Iterative Improvement: Program creation requires launching before you feel ready and improving based on feedback, rather than waiting for perfection.

From Individual Expertise to Systematic Knowledge Transfer: Your value shifts from what you know to how effectively you can teach others what you know.

From Time-Based Value to Outcome-Based Value: Students pay for transformation and results, not for hours of your time.

Risk Mitigation in Program Development

The Accelerator teaches nurses how to minimize the risks associated with program creation:

Start Small and Test: Launch with a small cohort to validate the concept before investing heavily in marketing or technology.

Maintain Consulting Income: Don't abandon proven revenue streams while building new ones. Use consulting success to fund and validate program development.

Focus on Proven Expertise: Create programs around knowledge you've already successfully applied, not theoretical concepts.

Price for Sustainability: Charge enough to make the program profitable even with smaller enrollment numbers.

Build on Existing Networks: Launch to professional connections who already know and trust your expertise.

The Compound Effect on Career and Impact

As Olivia discovered, creating successful programs doesn't just generate revenue—it compounds your professional reputation and career opportunities in ways that consulting alone cannot achieve:

Thought Leadership: Teaching positions you as an expert in your field, leading to speaking, writing, and media opportunities.

Network Expansion: Program students become professional connections across multiple organizations and geographic areas.

Innovation Opportunities: Teaching forces you to stay current with best practices and often leads to research and development opportunities.

Legacy Building: Programs create lasting impact that extends far beyond individual client relationships.

Wealth Acceleration: Successful programs often generate more income in a few months than years of traditional employment.

The transition from time-trading to empire-building represents the ultimate evolution of nursing expertise. It's the difference between being well-paid for your time and creating assets that generate wealth, impact, and legacy for years to come.

Wealth Work: Building Your Digital Empire Blueprint

Part 1: Expertise Audit and Program Identification

Your Unique Clinical Knowledge: List your top 3 areas of specialized nursing expertise:

1. _____

2. _____

3. _____

Problem Identification: For each expertise area, identify the specific problem it solves:

- Expertise 1 solves: _____
- Expertise 2 solves: _____
- Expertise 3 solves: _____

Market Validation Check: Answer these questions for your top expertise area:

- Have colleagues asked you to teach them this? ☐ Yes ☐ No
- Do you get consulting requests for this knowledge? ☐ Yes ☐ No
- Are there conferences/workshops on this topic? ☐ Yes ☐ No
- Would nurses pay to become confident in this area? ☐ Yes ☐ No

Target Audience Definition: Who specifically would benefit most from your expertise?

- Job titles: _____
- Experience level: _____
- Current challenges: _____
- Geographic location: _____

Part 2: Program Concept Development

Program Name and Positioning: Following Olivia's model, create your program concept:

Program Name: _____

Subtitle: _____

Target Audience: _____

Main Problem Solved: _____

Transformation Promise: _____

Program Structure Design:

- Program length: _____ weeks
- Session format: ☐ Group coaching ☐ Self-paced ☐ Hybrid
- Session frequency: ☐ Weekly ☐ Bi-weekly ☐ Other: _____
- Group size: ☐ 10-15 ☐ 20-25 ☐ 30+ people
- Additional support: ☐ Private group ☐ Resources ☐ 1:1 calls

Content Outline: Map your curriculum using this framework:

Week 1: _____

Week 2: _____

Week 3: _____

Week 4: _____

Week 5: _____

Week 6: _____

Week 7: _____

Week 8: _____

Part 3: Business Model and Pricing Strategy

Revenue Projections: Calculate potential income at different price points:

Conservative Pricing ($497):

- 10 students: $4,970
- 20 students: $9,940
- 30 students: $14,910

Market-Rate Pricing ($797):

- 10 students: $7,970
- 20 students: $15,940
- 30 students: $23,910

Premium Positioning ($997):

- 10 students: $9,970
- 20 students: $19,940
- 30 students: $29,910

Annual Revenue Potential: If you run 4 cohorts per year with 25 students each:

- At $497: $49,700 annually
- At $797: $79,700 annually
- At $997: $99,700 annually

Pricing Decision: Based on your expertise level and market research: **My program price will be: $_____ My target enrollment per cohort: _____ My projected annual revenue: $_____**

Part 4: Implementation Timeline

90-Day Launch Plan:

Days 1-30 (Foundation): ☐ Finalize program curriculum ☐ Choose technology platform (Kajabi, Teachable, etc.) ☐ Set up payment processing ☐ Create lead magnet ☐ Begin building email list

Days 31-60 (Marketing): ☐ Create content showcasing expertise ☐ Build waitlist through free masterclass ☐ Partner with nursing organizations ☐ Develop launch sequence emails ☐ Create program sales page

Days 61-90 (Launch): ☐ Open enrollment ☐ Conduct discovery calls with prospects ☐ Launch first cohort ☐ Gather testimonials and feedback ☐ Plan next cohort improvements

Part 5: Support and Acceleration Assessment

Current Business Knowledge: Rate yourself 1-10 in these areas:

- Online marketing: _____
- Program creation: _____
- Technology setup: _____
- Pricing strategy: _____
- Sales conversations: _____
- Community building: _____

Support Needs: Which areas would benefit most from coaching/community support?

1. _____

2. _____

3. _____

Accelerator Interest: Are you interested in learning more about intensive support for building your nursing business? □ Yes, I want to accelerate my timeline □ Maybe, I'd like more information □ No, I prefer to learn independently

Next Immediate Step: What is the single most important action you'll take this week to move toward creating your program?

Success Metric: How will you know your program is successful beyond just revenue?

Coming Next: In our final chapter, Olivia will step fully into her role as a leader and mentor, showing how individual transformation can spark systemic change in nursing. You'll discover how your wealth-building journey positions you to create lasting impact that extends far beyond your own financial success, and how the skills that make you wealthy can make the entire nursing profession stronger.

CHAPTER 11

YOUR REVOLUTION STARTS NOW

"The revolution you've been waiting for isn't coming from outside the profession—it's coming from nurses who refuse to accept financial limitation as the price of meaningful work."

Olivia's Story: Two Years Later

OLIVIA STOOD AT THE PODIUM IN THE MAIN AUDITORIUM OF THE National Nursing Convention, looking out at 800 nurses who had given up their Saturday morning to attend her session: "From Burnout to Breakthrough: Building Wealth Without Leaving Nursing."

Two and a half years ago, she'd been crying in a hospital parking garage, feeling trapped by circumstances she couldn't control. Today, she was the keynote speaker at the profession's largest annual gathering, sharing a message that was changing how nurses think about their careers and their worth.

The transformation metrics were staggering, even to her:

Financial Transformation:
- Net worth: $387,000 (from $15,000 starting point)
- Investment accounts: $67,000 and growing by $2,000 monthly
- Business income: $18,000-25,000 monthly through her consulting and education company

- Freedom Number timeline: Accelerated from 15 years to 7 years
- Financial stress level: Zero

Professional Transformation:
- Built a seven-figure consulting business specializing in ECMO education and nurse wealth coaching
- Speaks at 15-20 conferences annually
- Published articles in three major nursing journals
- Serves on the board of two nursing organizations
- Mentors 200+ nurses through her programs

Personal Transformation:
- Works 25-30 hours per week by choice
- Takes 8 weeks of vacation annually
- Energy level consistently 8-9 out of 10
- Relationship with Mickey stronger than ever
- Teaching Madison about money, investing, and self-worth from age 7

But the numbers only told part of the story. The real transformation was evident in how she carried herself, how she spoke about nursing, and how other nurses responded to her presence.

"How many of you have been told that good nurses don't focus on money?" she asked the audience.

Nearly every hand went up, accompanied by knowing laughter.

"I used to believe that too," Olivia continued. "I thought that wanting financial security somehow made me less caring, less dedicated, less... nursy. I was wrong. And that lie is costing our profession the best and brightest minds who leave nursing because they can't afford to stay."

She clicked to her next slide: a photo of her seven-year-old daughter Madison in a small business suit, holding a play microphone.

"This is my daughter Madison. Last week, she told her teacher that when she grows up, she wants to be a 'rich nurse who helps people and makes good money.' Not a nurse OR a businesswoman, but a nurse

AND a businesswoman. She can't imagine why anyone would think those things are mutually exclusive."

The audience laughed, but Olivia could see the shift in their expressions—the recognition that a new generation was watching how they handled the relationship between caring and earning.

"Madison has watched me transform from someone who worked overtime out of desperation to someone who chooses her work based on impact and fulfillment. She's seen me negotiate contracts, make investment decisions, and build a business—all while becoming a better nurse, not a worse one."

Olivia paused, looking out at the sea of faces. These were her people—exhausted, dedicated, undervalued professionals who had been told for too long that they should be grateful for scraps.

"I want to tell you about what happens when nurses stop accepting financial limitation. Not just for you, but for everyone whose life you touch."

She clicked to the next slide: testimonials from nurses who had worked with her over the past year.

"After implementing Olivia's strategies, I negotiated a $15,000 salary increase and started a side business that's now replacing my nursing income." —Sarah M., ICU Nurse

"I went from living paycheck to paycheck to having six months of expenses saved and $25,000 invested. My patients get the best of me now because I'm not distracted by financial stress." —Marcus R., ER Nurse

"I launched my consulting business and made $50,000 in my first year while working fewer hours. I finally feel like nursing is sustainable long-term." —Diana L., NICU Nurse

"These aren't anomalies," Olivia said. "These are the predictable results when nurses apply the same systematic thinking they use in patient care to their personal finances."

She told them about the WEALTH framework—not as theory, but as a lived experience that had transformed not just her bank account, but her entire relationship with nursing.

"When I started this journey, I thought I was just trying to pay my bills without working myself to death. What I discovered was that financial empowerment doesn't just change your life—it changes your capacity to serve others."

The audience was completely silent now, leaning forward.

"When you're not worried about money, you advocate more fearlessly for your patients. When you have financial options, you can choose assignments based on learning and growth rather than just survival. When you understand your true worth, you negotiate for working conditions that benefit not just you, but every nurse who comes after you."

She clicked to her final slide: a photo of the nurses she now employed in her business—five nurses who had built their own consulting practices under her mentorship, creating jobs and opportunities that hadn't existed before.

"This is what happens when nurses refuse to accept financial limitation. We don't just transform our own lives—we create new possibilities for the entire profession."

After her presentation, Olivia was surrounded by nurses wanting to know more. But one conversation stood out. A young nurse named Rebecca approached her with tears in her eyes.

"I've been thinking about leaving nursing," Rebecca said. "I love patient care, but I can't afford to stay. I have $80,000 in student loans, I'm working three jobs, and I still can't make ends meet. Hearing you speak... it's the first time I've felt hope that I could have both the career I love and the financial security I need."

Olivia handed Rebecca her card. "You absolutely can have both. But you have to stop believing the lie that caring and earning are opposites. They're not opposites—they're partners."

That evening, Olivia sat in her hotel room reflecting on the day. Her phone buzzed with messages from nurses who had attended her session, many already taking the first steps toward their own transformations.

Others were signing up for her online course or applying for her intensive coaching program.

But the message that made her smile came from Mickey: *"Madison watched your livestream during lunch. She said, 'Mommy is teaching nurses how to be rich like her.' I told her you're teaching them how to be smart with money so they can take better care of people. She said, 'Same thing.' Smart kid."*

Olivia laughed. Madison was right. It was the same thing.

As she prepared for bed, Olivia thought about the journey that had brought her to this moment. Every strategy she'd implemented, every mindset shift she'd made, every dollar she'd invested had compounded not just into personal wealth, but into the capacity to create systemic change.

The revolution had started with her own transformation, but it was scaling through every nurse whose life she touched, every workplace culture that shifted because of financially empowered nurses, every patient who received better care from nurses who were operating from abundance rather than desperation.

Two and a half years ago, she'd been one stressed nurse in a parking garage. Tonight, she was a leader in a movement that was changing how an entire profession thought about worth, wealth, and what was possible.

The revolution wasn't coming from outside nursing. It was coming from within, one transformed nurse at a time.

The Wealth Shift

Olivia's story isn't unique—it's replicable. Over the past several years, I've worked with nurses who have achieved career transformations. Some have built six-figure businesses. Others have achieved financial independence while remaining in bedside nursing. All have discovered that the skills that make them excellent nurses are the same skills that can make them wealthy.

But here's what I want you to understand: this isn't just about individual success stories. When nurses achieve financial empowerment, it creates ripple effects that transform the entire healthcare system.

What Changes When Nurses Build Wealth

Patient Care Improves: Nurses who aren't stressed about money are more present, more creative, and more willing to advocate fearlessly for their patients. Financial security eliminates the distraction of survival concerns, allowing complete focus on clinical excellence.

Workplace Culture Shifts: Financially empowered nurses don't accept toxic working conditions. They negotiate for better staffing ratios, safer environments, and policies that support both nurse wellbeing and patient outcomes. Their confidence creates positive pressure for systemic improvements.

The Profession Attracts Better Talent: When nursing becomes a path to genuine wealth building rather than just "stable employment," it attracts ambitious, entrepreneurial minds who might otherwise choose other careers. This elevates the entire profession's intellectual capital.

Innovation Accelerates: Nurses with financial resources and business acumen become healthcare entrepreneurs, creating solutions to problems they've identified through clinical experience. They fund research, develop technology, and launch companies that improve patient outcomes.

Nursing Leadership Expands: Financially independent nurses run for office, serve on corporate boards, and take executive positions in healthcare systems. They bring bedside perspective to high-level decision making, improving policies that affect both nurses and patients.

Healthcare Costs Decrease: When nurses understand business and finance, they identify inefficiencies and develop cost-effective solutions. Their clinical expertise combined with financial literacy creates innovations that improve outcomes while reducing expenses.

Why Healthcare Needs Wealthy Nurses

The current healthcare system is unsustainable. We're facing nursing shortages, burnout epidemics, and quality of care issues that threaten patient safety. The traditional solutions—recruiting more nurses, mandating overtime, offering small bonuses—aren't working as they don't address the root problem.

The root problem is that nursing has been positioned as a profession where you choose between caring for others and caring for yourself financially. This false choice is driving talented people away from nursing and keeping those who stay in survival mode rather than innovation mode.

We need nurses who understand that financial empowerment and patient advocacy aren't opposites—they're the same goal achieved through different means. We need nurses who can think strategically about both clinical outcomes and business sustainability. We need nurses who can innovate as a result of having the financial freedom to take risks.

Most importantly, we need nurses who can model for the next generation that caring for others and building wealth aren't just compatible—they're synergistic.

The Compound Effect of Individual Transformation

Every nurse who implements the WEALTH framework creates impact that extends far beyond their personal financial success:

Family Impact: Your children observe wealth-building behaviors and internalize abundance mindsets. Your spouse becomes more financially strategic. Your extended family seeks guidance and begins their own transformations.

Professional Impact: Your colleagues notice your increased confidence and competence. Your advocacy for better working conditions benefits everyone. Your example proves that transformation is possible.

Patient Impact: Your presence and advocacy improve because you're operating from abundance rather than desperation. Your clinical decisions are sharper because you're not distracted by financial stress.

Community Impact: Your volunteer time and charitable giving increase because you have resources to share. Your leadership in professional organizations elevates the entire nursing community.

Systemic Impact: Your success contributes to changing the narrative about nursing and money. Your innovations improve healthcare outcomes. Your mentorship creates more financially empowered nurses.

This is why individual transformation is actually a collective responsibility. When you build wealth as a nurse, you're not just improving your own life—you're contributing to the elevation of the entire profession.

The Choice That Defines Your Career

Right now, you might be at the same crossroads Olivia faced in that hospital parking garage two and a half years ago. You can continue accepting the status quo—the financial stress, the limited options, the belief that nurses can't be wealthy—or you can choose transformation.

But understand this: choosing transformation isn't just about you. It's about every patient whose care will improve because you're operating from abundance rather than scarcity. It's about every nurse who will be inspired by your example. It's about your children or nieces or nephews who are watching how you handle the relationship between work and worth.

The nursing profession needs you to choose transformation. Healthcare needs financially empowered nurses who can think strategically, advocate fearlessly, and innovate freely. Patients need nurses who aren't distracted by survival concerns but can focus completely on healing and care.

What This Journey Actually Requires

I want to be honest about what transformation actually takes, because Olivia's story might make it seem easier than it is. Building wealth as a nurse requires:

Mindset Work: You'll need to unlearn beliefs about money and nursing that have been reinforced by years of cultural conditioning. This takes consistent effort and often feels uncomfortable.

Strategic Thinking: You'll need to approach your finances with the same systematic rigor you bring to patient care. This means tracking, analyzing, and optimizing rather than hoping and guessing.

Delayed Gratification: You'll need to invest money that could be spent on immediate pleasures in order to build long-term wealth. This requires discipline and vision.

Risk Tolerance: You'll need to try new things—investments, side businesses, negotiations—that feel scary at first. Growth happens outside your comfort zone.

Persistence: You'll face setbacks, market downturns, failed attempts, and moments of doubt. Success requires continuing when stopping would be easier.

Community: You'll need support from other nurses who understand both the challenges and the possibilities. Transformation is difficult in isolation.

But here's what I know after working with hundreds of nurses: you already have every skill you need. The same abilities that make you an excellent nurse—systematic thinking, risk assessment, resource optimization, crisis management, and compassionate leadership—are exactly the skills that build lasting wealth.

You don't need to become someone different. You need to apply who you already are to an area of your life you've been neglecting.

Your Next Steps: From Reading to Revolution

Reading Olivia's story is inspiring, but inspiration without action is just entertainment. If you're serious about transformation, here's exactly what you need to do:

Week 1: Foundation Assessment

- Calculate your true net worth using the method from Chapter 3
- Track every expense for one week to understand your current spending patterns
- Complete the energy audit from Chapter 4 to identify your peak performance times
- Write your current money story and your new empowered money story from Chapter 2

Week 2: Immediate Optimization

- Open a high-yield savings account and set up automatic emergency fund transfers
- Research investment options and open your first investment account
- Audit your employee benefits and optimize your retirement contributions
- Calculate your true hourly wage including all costs of working

Week 3: Strategy Implementation

- Begin systematic investing with whatever amount you can sustain consistently
- Identify your most marketable nursing expertise and research monetization options
- Set up basic tracking systems for income, expenses, investments, and energy
- Create your first 90-day wealth-building goal

Week 4: Acceleration Planning

- Calculate your Freedom Number using the method from Chapter 7
- Develop a timeline for financial independence based on your current trajectory
- Identify three strategies that could accelerate your progress
- Create accountability systems and find community support

Ongoing: System Optimization

- Complete monthly financial reviews and adjust strategies based on results
- Continuously educate yourself about investing, business, and wealth building
- Network with other financially empowered nurses and healthcare professionals
- Track your progress and celebrate wins while adjusting for challenges

Advanced Support: The Nursing Wealthy Accelerator

If you're serious about accelerating your transformation and want the same kind of intensive support that helped Olivia scale her success, I've created the Nursing Wealthy Accelerator—a comprehensive coaching program designed specifically for nurses ready to transform their financial lives.

The Accelerator includes:

- **Systematic Wealth Building:** Step-by-step implementation of all WEALTH framework strategies with personalized guidance
- **Business Development Support:** Help launching and scaling expertise-based income streams
- **Investment Education:** Advanced strategies for healthcare professionals including sector-specific opportunities

- **Mindset Coaching:** Deep work on money beliefs and success psychology specific to nursing culture
- **Community Access:** Connection with other transforming nurses for support, accountability, and networking
- **Ongoing Support:** Monthly coaching calls, resource updates, and strategy refinements

The nurses who join the Accelerator typically achieve in 6-12 months what takes others 2-3 years to accomplish on their own. They build wealth faster, with more confidence, and with the support of a community that understands both their challenges and their potential.

But more importantly, they become leaders in the movement to transform nursing from a profession that accepts financial limitation to one that embraces strategic wealth building as a form of patient advocacy.

If you're ready to join this movement and want to accelerate your transformation with intensive support, you can learn more about the Accelerator at nursingwealthy.com/accelerator.

The Community That Sustains Transformation

One of the most important things I've learned from working with transforming nurses is that community makes the difference between temporary inspiration and lasting change. Olivia's success was accelerated by her connection with Cara and later with other nurses who shared her vision.

You need the same kind of community. Seek out:

- **Other nurses who are building wealth:** They understand your unique challenges and opportunities
- **Healthcare professionals with business experience:** They can provide mentorship and guidance
- **Investment and business education communities:** They offer knowledge and strategies you can adapt to nursing

- **Professional nursing organizations focused on leadership:** They provide platforms for growing your influence

Remember: transformation happens faster in community than in isolation. Don't try to do this alone.

The Legacy You're Creating

As you begin this journey, I want you to think beyond your own financial goals. Every step you take toward wealth building creates ripple effects that extend far beyond your bank account.

Your children, nieces and nephews are watching how you handle money and worth. Your colleagues are observing whether transformation is possible. Your patients are receiving care from someone who is either operating from abundance or scarcity. Your profession is being elevated or diminished by your example.

The wealth you build becomes a platform for impact. The confidence you gain becomes advocacy for others. The systems you create become models for replication. The success you achieve becomes proof that others can achieve it too.

You're building personal wealth. And, you're contributing to a revolution that's changing how nurses think about their worth, their possibilities, and their capacity to create positive change in healthcare.

Your Revolution Starts Now

Two and a half years ago, Olivia Wallace was sitting in a hospital parking garage, crying about money and feeling trapped by circumstances she couldn't control. She had no idea she was about to begin a transformation that would not only change her life but create ripple effects that would impact hundreds of other nurses, thousands of patients, and ultimately contribute to shifting the culture of an entire profession.

Olivia's story started with a moment of decision—a choice to reject the lie that nurses can't be wealthy and to begin implementing strategies that treated wealth building as seriously as patient care.

Your story starts with the same choice.

You can close this book and return to accepting financial limitation as the price of meaningful work. You can continue believing that wanting wealth somehow makes you less caring, less dedicated, less worthy of the nursing identity you've worked so hard to earn.

Or you can choose transformation.

You can choose to apply the same systematic excellence you bring to patient care to your personal finances. You can choose to value your expertise enough to monetize it appropriately. You can choose to build wealth not despite being a nurse, but because you're a nurse with unique skills, perspectives, and opportunities.

You can choose to become living proof that caring for others and building wealth aren't opposites—they're partners in creating the kind of life and career that allows you to serve from abundance rather than desperation.

The healthcare system desperately needs nurses who make this choice. Patients need advocates who aren't distracted by financial stress. Colleagues need examples of what's possible. The next generation of nurses needs role models who demonstrate that nursing can be both financially rewarding and deeply meaningful.

But most importantly, you need this transformation. Not just for the money, but for the confidence, the options, the freedom, and the capacity to create the kind of impact you became a nurse to create.

The strategies are proven. The framework is clear. The support is available. The only question remaining is: Will you choose transformation?

Your revolution doesn't start when conditions are perfect, when you have more time, when you feel more confident, or when someone gives you permission. Your revolution starts now, with the first small step toward treating your financial health with the same systematic care you provide to your patients.

Olivia's transformation began with calculating her true net worth and realizing she had more assets than she thought. Your transformation might begin with opening your first investment account, tracking your expenses for a week, or simply deciding that you deserve better than financial stress and limitation.

The revolution that's changing nursing doesn't require you to stop caring for others. It requires you to start caring for yourself with the same strategic excellence you bring to everything else that matters.

The nursing profession needs you to make this choice. Healthcare needs financially empowered nurses. Patients need advocates who operate from abundance. Your family needs the security and example that comes from strategic wealth building.

But beyond all of that, you need this transformation. You deserve to experience the confidence, freedom, and impact that come from refusing to accept financial limitation as the price of meaningful work.

The revolution starts with nurses who reject the false choice between caring and earning. It continues with nurses who implement systematic wealth-building strategies. It scales through nurses who mentor others and create new possibilities for the profession.

It starts with you. It starts today. It starts now.

Welcome to your revolution.

Ready to join the movement of financially empowered nurses who are transforming healthcare from positions of strength rather than scarcity? Your journey begins with a single step, and that step starts now.

*Visit **www.maryghazarian.com/nursingwealthy** to access free resources, connect with our community, and learn about intensive transformation support through the Nursing Wealthy Accelerator.*

The revolution you've been waiting for isn't coming from outside the profession—it's coming from nurses like you who refuse to accept that caring and wealth building are mutually exclusive.

Your transformation starts now.

THE WEALTHY NURSE TOOLKIT

"Having the right tools makes the difference between inspiration and implementation. This toolkit contains everything you need to transform your financial life using the strategies from this book."

TOOL #1: THE TRUE NET WORTH CALCULATOR

Standard Assets

Asset Category	Current Value
Checking Accounts	$_____
Savings Accounts	$_____
Investment Accounts	$_____
Taxable Investment Accounts	$_____
Real Estate Equity	$_____
Vehicles (current value)	$_____
Other Valuable Assets	$_____
TOTAL STANDARD ASSETS	$_____

Nursing-Specific Assets

Professional Asset	Estimated Value
Career Earning Potential (Annual salary × years left × 0.8)	$_____
Specialized Certifications Value	$_____
Professional Network Value	$_____
Expertise Portfolio Value	$_____
TOTAL NURSING ASSETS	$_____

Liabilities

Debt Category	Balance Owed
Credit Card Debt	$_____
Student Loans	$_____
Mortgage Balance	$_____
Car Loans	$_____
Personal Loans	$_____
Other Debts	$_____
TOTAL LIABILITIES	$_____

Net Worth Calculation

Standard Net Worth: Standard Assets - Liabilities = $_____

Total Nursing Net Worth: (Standard + Nursing Assets) - Liabilities =

$_____

TOOL #2: FREEDOM NUMBER CALCULATOR

Step 1: Calculate Annual Expenses

Expense Category	Monthly Amount	Annual Amount
Housing (rent/mortgage, insurance, taxes)	$_____	$_____
Transportation	$_____	$_____
Food & Household	$_____	$_____
Insurance (health, life, disability)	$_____	$_____
Debt Payments	$_____	$_____
Personal & Discretionary	$_____	$_____
TOTAL ANNUAL EXPENSES		$_____

Step 2: Apply Nursing Adjustments

- **Base Annual Expenses:** $_____
- **Minus Part-time Nursing Income Potential:** -$_____
- **Minus Professional Stability Buffer:** -$_____
- **ADJUSTED ANNUAL NEED:** $_____

Step 3: Calculate Freedom Number

- **Freedom Number:** Adjusted Annual Need × 25 = **$**_____
- **Traditional Freedom Number:** Total Annual Expenses × 25 = $_____
- **Nursing Advantage:** $_____ in reduced target

Step 4: Timeline Calculation

- **Current Total Assets:** $_____
- **Monthly Wealth Building:** $_____
- **Annual Wealth Building:** $_____ × 12 = $_____
- **Amount Still Needed:** Freedom Number - Current Assets = $_____
- **Years to Freedom:** Amount Needed ÷ Annual Wealth Building = _____ **years**

TOOL #3: TRUE HOURLY WAGE CALCULATOR

Total Employment Costs

Cost Category	Annual Amount
Work Clothes & Uniforms	$_____
Commuting Costs	$_____
Parking Fees	$_____
Meals at Work	$_____
Professional Licenses & Certifications	$_____
Continuing Education	$_____
Professional Memberships	$_____
Work-Related Childcare	$_____
Stress-Related Healthcare	$_____
Work Equipment/Supplies	$_____
TOTAL WORK COSTS	$_____

Time Investment

Time Category	Hours per Week	Hours per Year
Scheduled Work Hours	_____	_____
Commute Time	_____	_____
Unpaid Overtime	_____	_____
Work Preparation Time	_____	_____
Work-Related Education	_____	_____
TOTAL WORK TIME		_____

True Hourly Wage Calculation

- **Annual Gross Salary:** $_____
- **Minus Work Costs:** $_____
- **Net Income from Work:** $_____
- **Total Hours Invested:** _____ hours
- **TRUE HOURLY WAGE:** Net Income ÷ Total Hours = $_____ **per hour**

TOOL #4: ENERGY AUDIT TEMPLATE

Daily Energy Tracking

Track your energy every 2 hours for 7 days using a 1-10 scale

Time	Day 1	Day 2	Day 3	Day 4	Day 5	Day 6	Day 7	Average
6 AM	___	___	___	___	___	___	___	___
8 AM	___	___	___	___	___	___	___	___
10 AM	___	___	___	___	___	___	___	___
12 PM	___	___	___	___	___	___	___	___
2 PM	___	___	___	___	___	___	___	___
4 PM	___	___	___	___	___	___	___	___
6 PM	___	___	___	___	___	___	___	___
8 PM	___	___	___	___	___	___	___	___
10 PM	___	___	___	___	___	___	___	___

Energy Patterns Analysis

Peak Energy Times: _____

Low Energy Times: _____

Energy Drains: _____

Energy Boosters: _____

Wealth Work Schedule Optimization

High Energy Tasks (Schedule during peak times):

- Investment research and portfolio decisions
- Business development and client work
- Important financial negotiations
- Strategic planning and goal setting

Medium Energy Tasks (Schedule during moderate times):

- Routine bill paying and account monitoring
- Educational content consumption
- Networking and relationship building
- Administrative business tasks

Low Energy Tasks (Schedule during low times):

- Automated systems monitoring only
- Simple maintenance tasks
- Rest and recovery activities
- No important financial decisions

TOOL #5: EXPERTISE AUDIT CHECKLIST

Clinical Expertise Assessment

Specialized Knowledge Areas:

☐ _____ (Years of experience: _____)

☐ _____ (Years of experience: _____)

☐ _____ (Years of experience: _____)

Certifications and Advanced Training:

☐ _____ (Date obtained: _____)

☐ _____ (Date obtained: _____)

☐ _____ (Date obtained: _____)

Unique Experience:

☐ _____

☐ _____

☐ _____

Monetization Potential Assessment

For each expertise area, evaluate:

Expertise Area 1: _____

- **Problem it solves:** _____
- **Target audience:** _____
- **Urgency level (1-10):** _____
- **Your unique advantage:** _____
- **Market demand evidence:** _____
- **Potential hourly rate:** $_____

Expertise Area 2: _____

- ▦ **Problem it solves:** _____
- ▦ **Target audience:** _____
- ▦ **Urgency level (1-10):** _____
- ▦ **Your unique advantage:** _____
- ▦ **Market demand evidence:**_____
- ▦ **Potential hourly rate:** $_____

Expertise Area 3: _____

- ▦ **Problem it solves:** _____
- ▦ **Target audience:** _____
- ▦ **Urgency level (1-10):** _____
- ▦ **Your unique advantage:** _____
- ▦ **Market demand evidence:**_____
- ▦ **Potential hourly rate:** $_____

Expertise Ranking

Highest potential expertise: _____

Reason: _____

Next steps to monetize: _____

TOOL #6: 90-DAY WEALTH BUILDING SPRINT

Month 1: Foundation (Days 1-30)

Week 1: Assessment ☐ Complete True Net Worth calculation ☐ Complete Energy Audit ☐ Complete Expertise Audit ☐ Write new money story

Week 2: Optimization ☐ Open high-yield savings account or equivalent ☐ Automate emergency fund contributions ☐ Audit employee benefits ☐ Set up investment account with local provider

Week 3: Systems ☐ Begin systematic investing ☐ Set up expense tracking ☐ Create monthly review schedule ☐ Join nursing wealth community

Week 4: Planning ☐ Calculate Freedom Number ☐ Create 1-year financial goals ☐ Plan Month 2 priorities ☐ Celebrate Month 1 progress

Month 2: Acceleration (Days 31-60)

Week 5: Income Optimization ☐ Research salary benchmarks ☐ Plan salary negotiation approach ☐ Optimize current job benefits ☐ Explore overtime strategies

Week 6: Expertise Development ☐ Begin monetizing top expertise ☐ Create professional website/profile ☐ Network with potential clients ☐ Set premium hourly rates

Week 7: Investment Growth ☐ Increase investment contributions ☐ Research healthcare sector investments ☐ Optimize investment allocation ☐ Set up automatic rebalancing

Week 8: System Refinement ☐ Evaluate Month 2 progress ☐ Adjust strategies based on results ☐ Plan Month 3 priorities ☐ Update financial projections

Month 3: Scale (Days 61-90)

Week 9: Business Launch ☐ Launch first consulting service ☐ Create client acquisition system ☐ Set up business banking ☐ Establish professional processes

Week 10: Health Investment ☐ Implement health optimization plan ☐ Invest in energy-boosting tools ☐ Create sustainable self-care routine ☐ Track health ROI metrics

Week 11: Advanced Strategies ☐ Research advanced investment options ☐ Plan potential program creation ☐ Explore Nursing Wealthy Accelerator ☐ Build professional network

Week 12: Integration ☐ Complete 90-day assessment ☐ Document lessons learned ☐ Plan next 90 days ☐ Celebrate transformation progress

TOOL #7: MONTHLY FINANCIAL REVIEW TEMPLATE

Monthly Wealth Check-In

Review Date: _____

Financial Metrics

Metric	Last Month	This Month	Change
Net Worth	$_____	$_____	$_____
Investment Balance	$_____	$_____	$_____
Emergency Fund	$_____	$_____	$_____
Monthly Income	$_____	$_____	$_____
Monthly Expenses	$_____	$_____	$_____
Monthly Savings Rate	___%	___%	___%

Goal Progress

90-Day Goals:

☐ Goal 1: _____ (Status: _____)
☐ Goal 2: _____ (Status: _____)
☐ Goal 3: _____ (Status: _____)

Annual Goals:

☐ Goal 1: _____ (Progress: ____% complete)
☐ Goal 2: _____ (Progress: ____% complete)
☐ Goal 3: _____ (Progress: ____% complete)

Energy and Health Assessment

Average Energy Level (1-10): _____

Health Investment ROI: _____

Work-Life Balance (1-10): _____

Stress Level (1-10): _____

Business Development

Consulting Income: $_____

New Opportunities Identified: _____

Professional Development Completed: _____

Network Expansion: _____

Lessons Learned

What worked well this month:

1. _____

2. _____

3. _____

What needs improvement:

1. _____

2. _____

3. _____

Next Month's Priorities

Financial Focus: _____

Business Focus: _____

Health Focus: _____

Learning Focus:_____

TOOL #8: INVESTMENT RESEARCH GUIDE

Investment Basics for Nurses

This section provides educational information only and is not personalized investment advice. Consult with a qualified financial advisor for guidance specific to your situation.

Key Investment Principles

Diversification: Spread investments across different asset classes to reduce risk **Low Costs:** Minimize fees and expenses that eat into returns **Time Horizon:** Align investments with your timeline to financial independence **Risk Tolerance:** Match investments to your comfort level with market volatility **Regular Investing:** Consistent contributions often matter more than perfect timing

Common Asset Classes to Research

Equity Investments (Stocks):

- Individual company stocks
- Broad market index funds
- Sector-specific funds (including healthcare)
- International/global equity funds

Fixed Income Investments (Bonds):

- Government bonds
- Corporate bonds
- Bond index funds
- Treasury inflation-protected securities

Alternative Investments:

- Real Estate Investment Trusts (REITs)
- Commodities
- Infrastructure funds

Healthcare Sector Investment Considerations

For nurses interested in investing in what they know

Potential Advantages:

- Deep understanding of industry trends
- Insight into company operations and challenges
- Ability to evaluate innovation and competitive advantages

Important Considerations:

- Don't put all investments in one sector
- Healthcare sector can be volatile
- Consider both growth and value opportunities
- Research regulatory and policy impacts

Healthcare Investment Categories to Research:

- Medical device companies
- Pharmaceutical and biotechnology companies
- Healthcare technology and digital health
- Hospital and healthcare service providers
- Medical facility real estate investment trusts

Investment Platform Selection Criteria

Essential Features to Compare:

- Management fees and expense ratios
- Available investment options
- Minimum investment requirements
- Educational resources and research tools
- Customer service and support
- User interface and mobile access
- Account types offered (retirement accounts, taxable accounts)

Questions to Ask Potential Providers:

- What are the total costs of investing with your platform?
- What types of accounts can I open?
- Do you offer automatic investing and rebalancing?
- What educational resources do you provide?
- How do I access customer support?
- What research and analysis tools are available?

Getting Started with Investing

Step 1: Education ☐ Learn basic investment terminology ☐ Understand different account types available in your country ☐ Research tax implications of different investment strategies ☐ Consider taking an investment basics course

Step 2: Goal Setting ☐ Define your investment timeline ☐ Determine your risk tolerance ☐ Set specific financial targets ☐ Decide how much you can invest regularly

Step 3: Platform Research ☐ Compare fees across multiple providers ☐ Evaluate available investment options ☐ Test user interfaces and tools ☐ Read reviews and ratings

Step 4: Start Small ☐ Open account with chosen provider ☐ Begin with a small, manageable investment ☐ Set up automatic contributions ☐ Monitor and learn from your experience

Working with Financial Professionals

When to Consider Professional Help:

- You have complex financial situations
- You're uncomfortable making investment decisions
- You need help with tax planning
- You want comprehensive financial planning

Types of Financial Professionals:

- **Fee-Only Financial Advisors:** Paid only by client fees
- **Commission-Based Advisors:** Earn commissions on product sales
- **Fee-Based Advisors:** Combination of fees and commissions
- **Robo-Advisors:** Automated investment management services

Questions to Ask Any Financial Advisor:

- How are you compensated?
- What are your qualifications and certifications?
- What is your investment philosophy?
- How often will we review my portfolio?
- What services are included in your fees?

TOOL #9: PROGRAM CREATION BLUEPRINT

Program Development Checklist

Step 1: Concept Validation ☐ Problem clearly identified ☐ Target audience defined ☐ Market demand confirmed ☐ Competitive analysis completed ☐ Unique value proposition established

Step 2: Curriculum Development ☐ Learning objectives defined ☐ Module structure created ☐ Content outline completed ☐ Assessment methods planned ☐ Delivery format chosen

Step 3: Pricing Strategy ☐ Value-based pricing calculated ☐ Market pricing researched ☐ Payment options defined ☐ Refund policy established ☐ Pricing psychology applied

Step 4: Technology Setup ☐ Learning platform selected ☐ Payment processing configured ☐ Email marketing system setup ☐ Website/landing page created ☐ Analytics tracking implemented

Step 5: Marketing Plan ☐ Launch strategy developed ☐ Content marketing calendar created ☐ Social proof collected ☐ Email sequences written ☐ Referral system designed

Program Pricing Framework

Value-Based Pricing Calculation:

- **Problem cost to student:** $_____
- **Solution value to student:** $_____
- **Time savings value:** $_____
- **Career advancement value:** $_____
- **Total transformation value:** $_____
- **Program price (10-20% of value):** $_____

Market Positioning:

- **Budget Option:** $497-697
- **Premium Option:** $797-1,497
- **VIP/Advanced Option:** $1,497-2,997

Launch Timeline Template

8 Weeks Before Launch: ☐ Content creation begins ☐ Technology platform setup ☐ Marketing strategy finalized

6 Weeks Before Launch: ☐ Content creation 50% complete ☐ Beta testers recruited ☐ Landing page live

4 Weeks Before Launch: ☐ Content creation 80% complete ☐ Email sequence written ☐ Social proof collected

2 Weeks Before Launch: ☐ Content finalized ☐ Systems tested ☐ Launch sequence scheduled

Launch Week: ☐ Pre-launch content shared ☐ Enrollment opens ☐ Daily engagement and promotion

Post-Launch: ☐ Student onboarding ☐ Program delivery ☐ Feedback collection ☐ Next cohort planning

TOOL #10: RECOMMENDED RESOURCES

Essential Reading

Nursing Career Development:

- "Nursing Wisely: How to Build a Nursing Career that is Worthwhile, Interesting, Sustainable, Empowered, and Limitless by Putting Yourself First" by Mary Ghazarian
- "Nursing Intuition: How to Trust Your Gut, Save Your Sanity, and Survive Your Career" by Jennifer A Johnson RN
- "The Nurse's Guide to Innovation: Accelerating the Journey" by Bonnie Clipper et al.

Wealth Mindset

- "You Are a Badass at Making Money" by Jen Sincero
- "Get Rich, Lucky Bitch!" by Denis Duffield-Thomas

Business and Entrepreneurship

- "Who Not How" by Dan Sullivan and Dr. Benjamin Hardy
- "Buy Back Your Time" by Dan Martell
- "Million Dollar Weekend" by Noah Kagan and Tahl Raz
- "The 7 Habits of Highly Effective People" by Stephen R. Covey
- "The Obvious Choice" by Jonathan Goodman

Investing and Wealth Building

- "Financial Feminist" by Tori Dunlap
- "Rich Dad, Poor Dad" by Robert T. Kiyosaki

Recommended Platforms and Tools

Investment Platforms:

- Research reputable local investment platforms
- Compare fees and fund selections
- Consider robo-advisors for automated investing

Business Tools:

- **Website:** WordPress, Squarespace, Wix
- **Email Marketing:** ConvertKit, Mailchimp, Flodesk
- **Course Creation:** Kajabi, Teachable, Thinkific
- **Payment Processing:** Stripe, PayPal, local payment processors
- **Scheduling:** Calendly, Acuity Scheduling

Financial Management:

- **Budgeting:** YNAB, Mint, or local budgeting apps
- **Business Accounting:** QuickBooks, FreshBooks, or local alternatives
- **Investment Tracking:** Wealth Simple or other platform-specific tools

Professional Organizations

Nursing Leadership:

- American Organization for Nursing Leadership (AONL)
- American Nurses Association (ANA)
- Sigma Theta Tau International Honor Society
- International Council of Nurses (ICN)
- Canadian Nurses Association (CNA)
- Nurse Practitioner Association of Canada (NPAC)
- Society of Nurse Scientists Innovators Entrepreneurs & Leaders (SONSIEL)

Continuing Education

Financial Education:

- Local financial literacy programs
- Online investment education platforms
- Government financial education resources

Business Development:

- Small business development resources in your region
- Google Digital Marketing courses
- LinkedIn Learning business courses

Networking and Community

Online Communities:

- Nursing Wealthy Facebook Group
- LinkedIn nursing entrepreneurship groups

Professional Events:

- National nursing conferences
- Healthcare innovation summits
- Local nursing organization meetings

QUICK REFERENCE: IMPLEMENTATION CHECKLIST

Week 1: Foundation

☐ Calculate true net worth ☐ Complete energy audit ☐ Write new money story ☐ Open high-yield savings account

Week 2: Optimization

☐ Set up automatic investments ☐ Audit employee benefits ☐ Calculate true hourly wage ☐ Join investment platform

Week 3: Expertise

☐ Complete expertise audit ☐ Research monetization options ☐ Set premium rates ☐ Begin networking

Week 4: Systems

☐ Create tracking systems ☐ Set up monthly reviews ☐ Calculate Freedom Number ☐ Plan next 90 days

Monthly Ongoing:

☐ Complete financial review ☐ Adjust investment contributions ☐ Network and learn ☐ Track progress toward goals

Quarterly Assessments:

☐ Review and adjust strategy ☐ Increase investment rates ☐ Plan business development ☐ Celebrate progress

EMERGENCY FINANCIAL DECISION FRAMEWORK

When facing any financial choice, ask these questions:

1. **Will this increase or decrease my net worth in 5 years?**
2. **Am I making this decision from abundance or scarcity?**
3. **Does this align with my values and long-term goals?**
4. **What would the wealthy version of myself do?**
5. **Am I being strategic or just reactive?**

If you can't answer positively to at least 4 of these questions, wait 24 hours before making the decision.

This toolkit is designed to be your practical companion throughout your wealth-building journey. Keep it accessible, use it regularly, and adapt it to your unique circumstances. Remember: the best tool is the one you actually use consistently.

For updated resources and additional tools, visit:
www.maryghazarian.com/nursingwealthy

SELECTED WORKS CITED

American Nurses Association. "Healthy Nurse, Healthy Nation: Year Five Summary Report." 2022.

National Academy of Medicine. "Taking Action Against Clinician Burnout: A Systems Approach to Professional Well-Being." 2019.

Organisation for Economic Co-operation and Development. "Health at a Glance 2023: OECD Indicators." 2023.

ACKNOWLEDGEMENTS

A special thank you to members of my advanced reader team including:

Claude Latulippe
Sharlene Cumberbatch
Peyton Bond
Lori Fauquier — Telemedicine Chick
Haadiya Chaudhry
Kiran Patel, NP-PHC
Shelly Li, NP- PHC
Yvonne Breidenbach
Anas Abidrabbu
Kevin Zizzo, NP
JC Gimenez, Oncology Specialized Nurse
and Many More

YOUR REVOLUTION STARTS
Now

Build Your Foundation:

Read "Nursing Wisely" to create a
sustainable career that supports
wealth building.

Continue Your Transformation:

Get Free Resources and Learn About the Accelerator:
Visit **www.maryghazarian.com/nursingwealthy**
for calculators, templates, ongoing strategies, and
information about personalized coaching support.

STAY CONNECTED

www.maryghazarian.com/nursingwealthy

Your hub for wealth-
building resources,
community, and
transformation support

The nursing profession needs financially empowered leaders. Your
transformation proves what's possible when nurses refuse to accept
financial limitations.

Your next step starts today.

Help Other Nurses Find This Message:

If this book changed how you see your potential as a nurse, please leave
an Amazon review. Your words help other nurses discover that they
don't have to choose between caring for others and building wealth.

ABOUT THE AUTHOR

Mary Ghazarian MN NP-PHC is a Nurse Practitioner, entrepreneur, and advocate for nursing financial empowerment. After experiencing her own financial struggles, Mary discovered that traditional financial advice completely ignored the unique advantages and challenges that nurses face. This revelation sparked a transformation that led her to build successful businesses while remaining deeply connected to nursing practice.

Mary is the author of *Nursing Wisely* and *Nursing Wealthy* and has helped countless Nurses and Nurse Practitioners start and grow their own businesses. Through her speaking, writing, and coaching, Mary is leading a revolution that's changing how an entire profession thinks about money, worth, and what's possible for nurses who refuse to accept financial limitation as the price of meaningful work. She continues to practice as a Nurse Practitioner, proving daily that caring for patients and building wealth go hand in hand.

www.ingramcontent.com/pod-product-compliance
Lightning Source LLC
Chambersburg PA
CBHW031504180326
41458CB00044B/6690/J